EVERYTHING IS JUST THAT

Ian McCrorie

Pariyatti Press
an imprint of
Pariyatti Publishing
www.pariyatti.org

First published, 2024
ISBN: 978-1-68172-805-6 (hardback)
ISBN: 978-1-68172-785-1 (paperback)
ISBN: 978-1-68172-786-8 (PDF)
ISBN: 978-1-68172-787-5 (ePub)
ISBN: 978-1-68172-788-2 (Mobi)
Library of Congress Control Number: 2024952569

Image credits:

Cover	Dr. Geo Poland	P. 79	Hendrik Morkel (unsplash.com/@hendrikmorkel)
P. 4	Dan Dennis (unsplash.com/@cameramandan83)	P. 82	Eberhard Grossgasteiger (unsplash.com/@eberhardgross)
P. 11	Shivam Dewan (unsplash.com/@shivamdewan)	P. 95	Kerin Gedge (unsplash.com/@keringedge)
P. 16	Jan Meeus (unsplash.com/@janmeeus)	P. 98	Viktor Forgacs (unsplash.com/@sonance)
P. 19	Thibaut charp (unsplash.com/@tibs_pics)	P. 101	Wojciech Pacześ (unsplash.com/@wojtekpaczes)
P. 22	Sergio Capuzzimati (unsplash.com/@sergio_capuzzimati)	P. 108	Paolo Bendandi (unsplash.com/@paolobendandi)
P. 29	Dave Hoefler (unsplash.com/@iamthedave)	P. 111	Rutil Sharma (unsplash.com/@lumiaz)
P. 32	Charlotte Harrison (unsplash.com/@charlottelharrison)	P. 116	K8 (unsplash.com/@_k8_)
P. 35	James Wainscoat (unsplash.com/@tumbao1949)	P. 119	Rajat Verma (unsplash.com/@lifewithrajat)
P. 38	Gilberto Peralta Bocio (unsplash.com/@gilbertopb)	P. 126	John Towner (unsplash.com/@heytowner)
P. 41	Luc van Loon (unsplash.com/@lucvanloon)	P. 131	Jeet Dhanoa (unsplash.com/@jeetdhanoa)
P. 44	Luna Wang (unsplash.com/@lunawangjl)	P. 134	Patrycja Chociej (unsplash.com/@patrycja_chociej)
P. 47	Polina Kuzovkova (unsplash.com/@p_kuzovkova)	P. 137	Jeremy Bishop (unsplash.com/@jeremybishop)
P. 54	Casey Horner (unsplash.com/@mischievous_penguins)	P. 144	Ganapathy Kumar (unsplash.com/@gkumar2175)
P. 59	Jean Wimmerlin (unsplash.com/@jwimmerli)	P. 147	Max Ducourneau (unsplash.com/@maxdcrn)
P. 68	Milada Vigerova (unsplash.com/@milada_vigerova)	P. 152	Jennifer Grismer (unsplash.com/@jennifergrismer)
P. 73	Dillon Pena (unsplash.com/@dillonpena)	P. 155	Shelter (unsplash.com/@shelter)
P. 76	Mark Olsen (unsplash.com/@markolsen)	P. 158	Chris Ensey (unsplash.com/@censey)
		P. 161	Kier in Sight Archives (unsplash.com/@kierinsightarchives)

To my family
forever and always

Also by Ian McCrorie

A Lifetime Doing Nothing (2021)
Children of Silence and Slow Time (2012)
The Moon Appears When the Water is Still (2003)

As to me I know nothing else but miracles ...

Walt Whitman

Long fed on boundless hopes, O race of man,
How angrily thou spurn'st all simpler fare!

Matthew Arnold

Introduction

The ceramic bowl I use for my morning oatmeal is chipped, sporting a large divot on its rim. To some, this disfiguration might destine it for a recycling bin. But I don't reject it. It is holding on, proudly so I might add, and not appreciative of the "damaged goods" label. This respect for the chipped, the antiquated, the aged and the damaged is honored in Japan as *wabi*. And as I contemplated this honorary level of recognition from Zen, I realized my chipped bowl was not the only example in my life of *wabi*. I still wear Kodiak work boots, presently paint-spotted with frayed laces, purchased with my first pay check in 1971. As well, my mucking-about-in-the-house sweater, originally the lining of a winter jacket, is over twenty years old. I wear a fedora that has seen me through thirty years of monsoons and forest treks in Europe and Asia. And I have a 160-year-old clock that stopped working, as did I, twenty years ago, though it is spot on twice a day, a feat I seldom accomplish according to my sons. But back to my chipped ceramic bowl—I respect it because it reflects the reality of human life. It continues to sort of tick along accompanied by an unseen but ominous fault line running through it. More to the point, my bowl didn't appear to give any undue attention to its chip. It simply gets on with bowling without getting distracted by a sense of impending doom. In life when you free yourself from the usual self-tirade of negative thinking and habits and emotions and reactions concerning your obvious chips, then they lose their power and remain just what they are. Everything and everyone is chipped and this is perfect in the sense that it is not necessary to cover them up with false bravado, with layers of makeup or with a victim's resignation. Everything that arises in the body or in the mind is just what it is. No need to make a big fuss about it. Some chips are already quite painful by themselves. There is no need to add more confusion and suffering. Better to understand that everything is just that. Over a thousand years ago Zen poets and monks wrote haiku with that same attitude, stripping away any extraneous emotional or descriptive artifice. Their poems spoke truth to life, chips and all. A favorite example of mine was penned by Basho (1644–1694).

The old pond
A frog jumps
Plop!

The word sums up the event perfectly. *Plop* is unambiguous. It is a sound, devoid of value or point of view. Basho throws no light on the frog's innermost thoughts, his intentions or his political leanings, and this is not simply because he has used up all his syllables. Such intellectualizing muddies the water and does not change reality one iota. I mean damn it all, man, the frog plopped! More importantly, plopping down is what we humans do best, when we are tired, for instance. And when you think about frogs and humans, both also stick out their tongues, at most times for different reasons. Our basic nature, in Zen called Buddha-nature, is found in everything — frogs, humans, trees, rocks. Haiku breathe life into these simple things just as they are, without drawing any conclusion or stating any premise. Furthermore, it stands to reason that Zen monks who see everything as just that, would produce poetry using as few words and/ or syllables as possible. With haiku, the template to aim for is the 5-7-5 syllable structure. This is difficult enough to do in Japanese, a language devoid of articles such as "the", "a", etc., making it even more challenging in English. Shiki, a nineteenth century haiku master, alluded to this restrictive adherence to form in the following poem.

forests and streams
much more than
seventeen syllables

It is important to honor the tradition of Basho not so much by adhering to a form but by maintaining the spirit of Basho and so many other masters, who breathed life into simple things. And it is this spirit of Basho which I endeavor to adhere to, his straightforward linking of meditation, poverty, isolation and simplicity into a literal snapshot capturing a profound miraculous moment in time. This linking of Zen (meditation) and poetry is the essence of haiku, forever together, and called *zenshi ichimi* in Japanese, either poetic meditation or meditative poetry. Clark Strand writes, haiku is "in many ways the most concrete and most perceptually grounded form of poetry, also the most inward." Haiku dispenses with description, opinions and, like Joe Friday on the old television detective show "Dragnet", asks for "Just the facts, ma'am, just the facts." Haiku avoids explanation and allows the things in the poems to speak for themselves. Though Zen monks established a quintessential art form, other schools and traditions followed suit. My own Theravadin teacher, S.N. Goenka, wrote two-line Rajasthani *dohas*, expressing Dhamma in the same straight forward, everyday way of haiku.

Lose not peace for joy and grief
Both, like day and night are brief

It seems undeniable to me that haiku-like poetry and meditation are one and the same — the former being the literate expression of the insights of the latter. This theory equally applies to secular spiritualists such as William Carlos Williams who said, "No ideas, but in things." This reverence for the everyday miracle of things just as they are, abides in the work of Walt Whitman, to wit the following triplet, a haiku by any other name:

But I am done with apple-picking now
Essence of winter sleep is on the night
The scent of apples: I am drifting off.

Everything and everyone is chipped, an obvious surface indication of weakened underlying structural tendencies, fault lines if you will, that the Buddha referred to as *sankharas*. Our *sankharas* are a seismic conditioning of epic proportions, twisting all our thoughts, actions and emotions. No being is spared; not even a Buddha. He was so troubled by these omnipresent fault lines; he left his home and family to find an answer. And he did so many years later sitting under a Banyan tree and then spent his adult life as a homeless mendicant spreading the good news that our chipped nature need not result in inevitable catastrophes. More to the point, there are steps to mitigate the fault line's hold over us. Our chips are manifestations of this hidden, subconscious conditioning. It proves problematic when we think it defines us, when we feel this is the way we are and always will be. The Buddha outlined a Noble Eightfold Path to eradicate the root cause of our suffering. This is a long, gradual process often leading to a flash of understanding, a dissolution of solidity. The Theravadin schools called this *bhanga*, in Zen it is *kensho*. The essence of this profound insight taps into the unconditioned mind, so called as it is empty of all the conditioning and impediments. Then and only then, everything that arises in the mind and the body is clearly seen without conditioning, just as it is and everything is just that.

The Buddha was not a God
He was a human being
That was enough
He experienced
Sights
Sounds
Smells
Tastes
Feelings
Thoughts
Just as you and I do
With all their auxiliary conditioning
He too had a lot of baggage to unpack
This took him about seven years
After his enlightenment
He understood all those
Sights, sounds, smells, tastes, feelings, thoughts
Were just that
Nothing more
No need to get all bent out of shape
No need to get enraged or elated
They weren't trying to get your goat
To send you off into paroxysms
Of tears or joy all day long
They just
See
Hear
Smell
Taste
Feel
Think
And the mind's role
Is simply to know that
Everything is just that.
Unconditioned
And extremely beautiful

Great blue heron standing
On a cedar raft -
White-capped waves bowing in rhythm

                                    I am old now
                      I wish I could say to my father
                    Unspoken words I only now feel

New Year's Day
Old woman fills her car trunk
With discounted Christmas ornaments and hope

                        In winter our street disappears
                      House boats float on cumulus seas
                                  Moving home snowly

Nobody doing nothing
Opens the gate to the deathless
Kindness lights the path to further

                                    Wanderer not lost
                          Found what was always there
                              Once he stopped looking

My father, sergeant-major Toronto-Scottish,
Spent six years overseas trying not to die
My mother, insurance executive secretary
Spent six years waiting
Finally married and had a child
Living in a three-story walk-up
Landlord also owned a movie theater
Every year he replaced the movie theater carpeting
Which he then cut and pasted in our hallways
Where, as a result, it smelled all the time of popcorn.
My Aunt lived in one apartment
We lived right above her
The occupants of the remaining
Four units were all single ladies
Waiting for their soldier boyfriends to come home
To join this sorority of single sisters.
My mother found herself
Staring at the rapidly closing window
Of her child-bearing years
I truly was the second coming
I had five surrogate mothers
All using me as a trial run
For what they hoped to be
Their own large family
I was constantly passed from my mother
To any number of mothers-to-be
Hence today my love of football
I was love-immersed
Every work day my father
Would stroller me to a nearby park
Where he would read his newspaper
And simply wait for help to arrive.
Not many babies were born during the war
So, I didn't have to wait long until
A giggle of young girls
Would come by to play with me.
I never felt anything but love

From family, from friends
And even strangers
I simply expected love
I thought that was how we bipedal apes behaved
And I still feel that way today

Old paint-splattered boots
Familiar like a mother's smile
Still carry these fragile bones to the workbench

Aged mother stares all day at the tree
As she lies in bed, waiting -
Maple angels comfort all souls

Never late on snow days
Pushing cars and each other
Everything dappled in white laughter

At Tisarana Forest Monastery
Buddhas young and old
Prostrate before majestic maples

In silence I sit
Receiving answers
To questions I didn't know I had

Uranus spins on its side
Hit by a rock eons ago
In a playground dispute

Breathe in, breathe out
Again...and again
Until you give up
Because you can't do it
Just let it be
Let the breath do the breathing
Now you are alive
You are free
You are the sound of silence
Open to all the wonders of the universe
Right here in front of you
Under your nose
Even under your feet
The miracles of small things
The oft-overlooked
The neglected, the unpraised
The underwhelmed,
The dejected, the broken
The worn down, the worn out
The magnificence of the mountain
In the anthill
The beauty of the rainbow
In the puddle beneath your feet
Why wait for a heaven
When every day a paradise
Awakens before your very eyes
All beginning with a single breath
Silence in, silence out

The wind blows the snow
Into smoky swirly squalls
Setting fire to icicles

No one walks
Across the bridge
This snowy eve

.

Gnarly twisted cedars
Extend from shoreline rocks
"Persevere" the frogs croak

Morning boreal lake
Mirror still
My awe making no waves

Snow-crunched-underfoot backbeats
Owl in a pine tree
Moon spotlights a winter sonata

The world overwhelms
I seek refuge
In water buffalo mind

You can't fix yourself
Because you aren't broken
You can't heal yourself
Because you aren't sick
You can't correct yourself
Because you aren't a problem
Sit quietly
Watch the mind,
The figuring out mind,
The judging mind
The mad-as-a-hatter mind,
Conditioned, contriving, contrary
Condescending, convoluted mind
Conning you that you aren't a Buddha.

✿

We are learning to walk
Without crutches
That is why we stumble
We trip, we fall down
We fail again and again
"Start again" is our mantra

✿

Our life, warts and all
One big mistake
Is there all the time
It doesn't run away
From the devastation
There to be experienced anew
As perfect
Again, and again
For the first time

The moonlit rink is lonely this late
Dreams of goals to come
Cheered on by the echo of skates

                                    If everyone fears the other
                                      There is no other to fear
                                          I, you, all are other

Peace begins after the discourse
Kindness arises after meditation
In deeds only, is good done

                                          La Ilaha ILallah
                                          There is no God
                                    There is nothing but God

Winter sleeping to the lullaby of dump trucks
Piling snow along the river
Morning, presto! new toboggan hills

                              Eleven years old delivering newspapers
                                          To elderly spinsters
                                    Smelling of cabbage and toast

Live an in-between life
'Twixt this and that
Yours and mine
Same and different
Native and refugee
Inside and outside
Us and them
Leaders and followers
Straddle the fulcrum
With arms outstretched
Welcoming polar opposites
Into your embrace.

❦

Near the Mekong
In northeast Issan
I went on alms round
During the monsoon season
The sun had just risen
As we set off to collect
Dana, our only food for the day
I felt honored to carry
The excess food
That wouldn't fit
In the monks' bowls.
I didn't smile
I kept my eyes downcast
I was holy
I was euphorically spiritual
My mind was in the clouds.

❦

The monks walked a few miles that day
Barefoot by tradition
The path was very muddy and slippery
I chanced to look up
And saw all the monks smiling
Enjoying themselves
Feeling a lot more oozy than holy
Perhaps the true path
Is more muddy and slippery
Maybe you learn more falling on your face
Than with your holy head in the clouds
Slip sliding away, baby

Before clocks
Was anyone late?
Time to find out

My entire life
One giant mistake
I stand uncorrected, and laugh

Let water buffalo mind
Show the path to peace -
Beast of unburden I say

Worn and trembly
Writing table and old worthless poet
Shake, rattle and roll together

He who knows does not speak
I never shut up
Teaching my sons how not to be

The wind reveals mouse brown muck
Walking leaves no footprints
Just the echo of thunder

At eighteen I took to the road
What joy driving the great boreal highway
No destination and no schedule
Like a rolling stone
Through the space-time continuum
Comin' up hard at the Pacific
Turned around and
Did it again, backwards
We were just kids
Livin' on KD, coffee, toast
And the kindness of strangers
But old enough to know
We knew nothing
And basking in our naive ignorance
That life was to be lived
Without regrets and hopes

At night in bed
I stretch out my feet
Until they touch my wife's.
Oh good, I am still married
But who is this
Lucky, lucky girl?
I giggle to myself and bow
As my audience of one
Sleeps.

Why one God?
Many Gods would be better
They'd be busy
Keeping an eye on each other
Leaving us alone
To follow our true religion
Being alive in this moment to the wonder and awe
Of it all

In the winter sleeping to the sounds of snow trucks
At the summer cottage a squirrel runs across the roof
Waking me from a dream of winter

You, Buddha, see yourself
Wipe off the dust
Ah, how the triple gem sparkles

There is nothing holy in enlightenment
Just a lot of space
Why spoil it with hopes and dreams?

Some think to go there
Others believe it is here
Stop looking, it is found

Temple gong wakes the sun
Pond of lotus flowers
Open to pay their respects

Running in the winter
Breathing through icicles
Home, melting into puddles

We moved to a rent-subsidized
Veterans-only housing project
When I was two. It was wonderful
There were 250 plus apartments
Distributed between 50 plus 3 story buildings
And separated by 3 playing fields.
Every apartment contained
The essential vet, his wife
And at least two children
Overnight I had 500 playmates
Within walking distance
All about my age
I never had a playdate
Never phoned a friend
Never walked to school by myself
I simply went outside
Whoever was there was whom
I talked to
I played with
I walked with
I expected whoever was outside would be a friend
A friend defined as the person you met outside
I lived in a ten-acre tautology
One summer day some of us were sitting outside
With nothing to do
Lalage suggested we go exploring
In the giant field right at my back door
We spent our days on the field
It was barren
What treasures could there be out there?
Lalage was the oldest so by law, the boss
So, explore, we did. All afternoon
When Mom called me for dinner
I couldn't wait to show her my loot:

3 pieces of string, some candy wrappers, a penny
2 cigarette butts, a part of a hockey puck
A veritable treasure of hidden gems that others had overlooked
And it was right there in front of their eyes
I still feel that way to this day
Myriad miracles of small things hiding right in plain sight
And we have but to put on our secret treasure-finding goggles
And open our eyes

Mist rising from the pond
Sound of shakuhachi
Asleep still, I am temple-sent

Zen untangles the self
From its masquerade
It is simply this

Storm passing across lake
Wood-warmed hill top cottage
Refuge cave for vagabond poets

Dragonflies mating on my canoe
Spider searching for his web
Ubering brothers on the River Styx

Now is the perfect harmony
Where past and future meet
Beyond the duality of self and other

This is not this, unless it is that
Only when the two are one
Are they truly two

Truth is an open secret.
Open because it is right in front of you
Secret because no one will tell you where it is
If you look too hard
You push it away
If you don't look
You'll never understand
Your answers
Which are always wrong
If you ask the wrong question
Because there is no question.

❦

He threw away his life
Being successful
Wealth was all he had,
Poor man
He drove a Porsche
Only in the summer
When it wasn't raining
He parked it far from other cars
Alarms go off
If anyone in that zip code sneezes
It sleeps in a heated garage
Under a blanket
Made from baby minks
I take a bus
And try not to gloat.

❦

Awareness isn't difficult.
Persistent awareness is something else again
It is why we need to practise
From time to time
Like a concert pianist
Who plays scales every morning
Staying nimble
Building muscle memory
Before he tackles Liszt

Where there are humans
You'll find mosquitoes
And saints

There is gold in them thar hills
Only he who desires it not
Finds it

Cardinal on a snowbank
Come to say goodbye
Or hello

I secure my garbage can
From foraging racoons
What can I share if not this?
Aren't racoons the ultimate recyclers?

Mosquitoes swarming
What do they want
With my aged blood?

You need not make peace with God
If you never quarreled
Inshallah

To really suffer
Hold on! Hold on!
To all your beliefs
To all your hopes and dreams
To all your wants and fears
To all you think you are
"I am this, I am not that"
"No, your honor, I am not that kind of person"
We tilt our cardboard lances
At the windmills of our minds
And revel in our proclamations
Of chivalry and honor.
We hone our personality
To be liked, admired and respected
Suffering is just that
Holding on to our conditioned selves
Canonizing our sundry incarnations of hope.
Let it all go
Wave goodbye
There you've lost everything
You are nobody
Doing nothing
No more raging against the dying of the light.
Let it all go
Now, just where did I put my suffering?

❦

Sitting on the morning bus on route to a desk job
At Acme Insurance, wearing a suit and tie
Your briefcase on your lap
Humming "Yesterday" as you tip your fedora
To your fellow passengers
You are Buddha
You are aware of the majesty and awe
Of this moment
You are not trapped in pursuit of

The perfect monastic environment
The perfect robes, the perfect chanting,
The perfect humble smile.
Humility, Spirituality, Religiosity
And their opposites
Are also conditioned habits

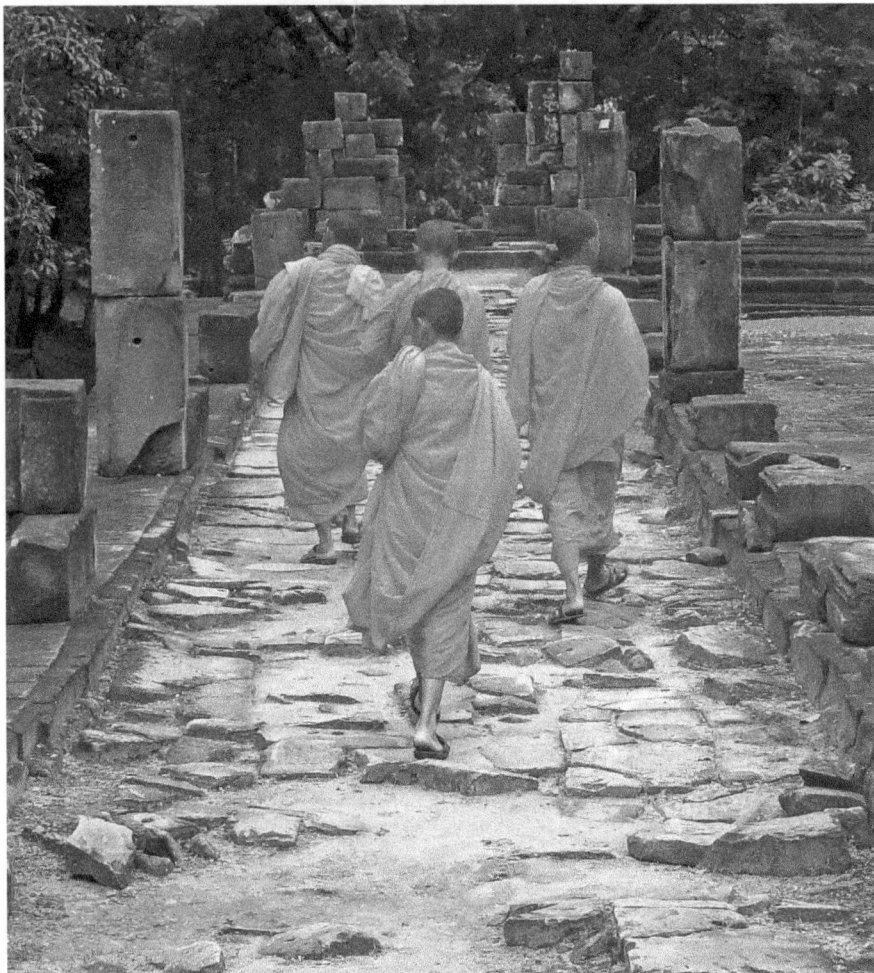

Sun in the sky
Earth below my feet
Today, enough

                                    Lost in the dark
                    Time is ripe to focus on moonlight
                          Streaming through the branches

The caw of the mighty crow
The pips of baby swallows
All under the eaves of heaven

                          Deer trapped in barbed wire fence
                     Released gingerly with wire cutters
                                His leap - "Thank you"

Crying
Know the tears are falling
And they are wet. Just that.

                                    The space between
                     Gives meaning to a string of letters
                          Truth arises only in emptiness

Lao Tzu advised us to learn to unlearn
Unlearn all that you have absorbed
All your conditioned responses
To various and sundry stimuli
Following the leads of your parents,
Your elders, your teachers, your friends
Your heroes, influencers, podcasters,
Websites,
Anybody and Anything.
Empty our mental shelves of all the detritus
Let it all go
Until everything is experienced as just that
Only then can you act or not act wisely.
No one doing nothing
Going nowhere
Walking on a beach leaving no footprints.

❧

For many years I traveled
To all the realms of gold
Hoping to discover the truth
Slowly I realized I already
Knew all I needed to know
That what I sought
Was the seeking.

❧

With less you are content
With more, you are confused
Misery abides with many keys
And a plethora of choices
Being true to yourself is futile
If your truth is conditioned
What is the point of saving face
If our face goes unseen behind a mask

You can't organize
A better world when
Your bedroom is a mess

Craving knows no end
Few stop at a billion
Or one wife

Nature never regrets nor hopes
Rice in the pot, wood in the stove
Anxiety and Elvis have left the building

Zen sidesteps the rational
Breaks the mold of linearity
Intellect implodes when space/time collide

Rejoice with he who weeps
Weep with he who rejoices
They are both fools

Do not ask foolish questions
Why not?
Silence! Have a corn chip

Even not to choose
Is to choose
The road forks
Now what?

❧

These words are not the truth
At best they are the finger
Pointing at the moon
They are not the moon
They can't teach you anything
If your heart isn't open
The heart has to be your Guru
The heart has to teach you itself.

❧

Don't take your life personally
Stop interjecting color commentary
Into every sight
Sound
Smell
Taste
Feeling
Thought
Conditioning every subsequent
Sight
Sound
Smell
Taste
Feeling
Thought
On and on it goes
The Buddha is clear
Everything is just that
As it is and no more
Everything else is just so much window dressing
You best keep out of it

Life rests between relative and absolute
Gaze at the stars
But lock your car in the garage at night

The caterpillar sheds his cocoon
He trusts his Buddha-nature
Behold! I can fly!

No birth without death
No death without birth
Just suchness between Alpha and Omega

Deliver us from all our sins
And our virtues-
Brothers of the same fodder

There is great danger
To think you understand something
Liberation is to know Nothing

How do I get enlightened?
Go and wash your dish
I don't understand?
Then wash your socks as well

Looking for the answer
Assumes there is an eternal question
There is no question
There is no problem
There is nothing to seek
Unfortunately, only serious seekers find this out
Everything is just that
Everything is just so
Live a long enough life
It is like watching summer reruns
You've seen it all before
Life is one big mistake
To be born is to put your foot
In the bait bucket
And spend the rest of your life
Laughing as you hop around
Sometimes falling
In horse manure
Other times falling
In a bed of roses
What difference does it make
You still can't remove your foot
From the bait bucket.

Somehow years ago
I got scattered all over the place
I set about making myself whole again
Not necessarily better, or wiser
Or kinder. Just together
In one whole piece,
All my stuff right
Where I can see it.
I was a well-organized closet
Marie Kondo would be so proud.

I think I am a Capricorn
I have no idea what house
My moon is in.
However, I do know
My son doesn't rise till noon
On the weekend

I take my tea
With Haydn and oatmeal cookies
Walkin' on the wild side, baby
For this old mendicant

If you carry a watch
No need to ask strangers for the time
Enlightenment is like this

Dew on the leaves of grass
Morning bird song
Beseeching me to lay down my burden and sing

There can be no greater joy
Than the laughter of my sons
At my wife's insulting spoonerism - Mozo Boron

A murder of crows gathers in my pine tree
An extended family I wonder
Celebrating National Carrion Day?

A clever man knows
What he knows
A wise man knows
What he does not know

I identify with the quiet outcasts
Who treasure the well-crafted
But old and somewhat broken
Who sit at the back
Let others go first
Comrades who frequent small bookstores
Vinyl record shops, one bay garages
Run by a guy named Moe
I seek comfort in those
With an easy smile
Who speak gently, are parsimonious
Listen well
And treasure what we have lost

If you think back that you shoulda
Remember too that you coulda
Now you wish that you woulda
Welcome to the Carousel of Repetitive Regrets
Climb aboard,
The Carousel never stops
Going faster and faster
The music getting louder and louder
You want to leave the ride
You can't
It has you in its grasp
The more you dwell on the regret
The faster and louder
Is the ride
Give up
Surrender
Forgive yourself
The ride slows
It quiets down
It becomes white noise
It is okay

If it lasts forever
That is fine
And once you really
Just accept
That it may endure
For your whole life
It dissolves

The practise of meditation
Is to patiently welcome
What we most wish to shut out

Dhamma is a boat
That floats on a
Tempestuous sea of problems
Without problems the boat is becalmed

By the time you
Explain the sunrise
You've missed it

This way, that way ends
In the same dead end
Better to take the path that goes nowhere

Is Dhamma the mist
That sits atop the mountain
Or the mountain itself?

Seeking the truth is futile
Until you cease basking in the profundity
Of your own opinions
At least, that's how I see it

Thich Nhat Hanh called it "Habit Energy"
Christians named it "The Devil"
Even though we know we will regret
Doing, speaking, reacting or thinking
In an acrimonious way
We seem powerless to its
Come hither beckoning
From where does this compulsion
To self-sabotage come from?
Who knows?
Who cares?
It is a waste of energy
To psychoanalyze its birth place.
And what difference would it really make
To find out it was my great grandmother
Who first scolded me for slurping my soup?
My habit energy remains intact
Every time I detect a slurp
Overpowered by such anger
I want to strangle the miscreant
Though I walk away,
Take a bus to the next town
Walk up a mountain
Sit in a cave
Put in my earbuds
Tune in Metallica
Top volume
Still, I hear slurping!
Habit Energies lessen only
When we smile and understand:
Slurping is simply noise vibrations
On the eardrum.

I am held hostage by my habits
I suffer from "Stockholm Syndrome"
Falling in love with these powerful forces
Convinced these repetitive habit energies
Reflect the real me
Over time I identify with the interlopers
Sublimating the unconditioned mind
Quietly residing inside since before I was born

After waking, I look outside
Sometimes I spot a haiku
Sitting there, patiently waiting

Mister cicada
If you didn't screech so much
It would not be so hot

Hineni
"I am ready, Lord
To die now, if it be time"

In the natural mind
There is no rejection, no acceptance
Like a child looking at a Rothko

Kalyana mitta
A benevolent friend
Someone you can phone
At three a.m.

A life of solitude
Is best enjoyed
With family and good friends

I have spent decades
On my cushion
In silent solitude
In humid jungles
Near the Mekong
In the deserts of Rajasthan
In Korean temples
And Hindu ashrams
I have chanted mantras
Experienced *shaktipat*
Practiced mindfulness
Vipassana Zazen Shikantaza
All trying to get somewhere
Doing anything it takes
To get there
It all led to frustration
I gave up
And perhaps this was the goal
Of these techniques
To have you surrender
To bow to the truth
To give up
The trying to get somewhere
To give up hoping for *kensho*
To let go of the need to have an answer
To let go of the need to succeed
Eyes closed, eyes open
Doing nothing. Going nowhere.

✿

In the film "The Karate Kid"
Daniel LaRusso is instructed
By Mr. Miyagi, his *sensei*,
To wax his collection of vintage cars with a circular motion
"Wax on, left hand, wax off, right hand"
Hour after hour, day after day

Daniel becomes frustrated
Wanting to learn real karate
Sensei attacks Daniel
Telling him to block his moves
"Wax on! Wax off"
Days of frustration leading to success.
Sound familiar?

Too many spend their days
Getting ready to live -
Somnambulists flailing away in the dark

Smell of asphalt after summer rain
Swimming at Duchie's Hole
Three-story walk-up - my St. Bart's

Live your life
As if you have no choice
But to live your life

Good news! Are you certain?
Bad news! Are you positive?
Wait and see. Wait and see

The end of something pleasant
Is not necessarily something unpleasant
It is just that

What is hope
But fear shrouded
In sheep's clothing

For this one moment
Feel what you are feeling
Immerse your mind into that feeling
You are that feeling
And that feeling is just that
A feeling
It did not arise
To put you in bliss
It does not have a purpose
It did not want to get your attention
To upset your apple cart
It is just that
You with a plethora
Of letters after your name
With citations and awards on your walls
Don't need to get involved
With this feeling.
It doesn't need to be
Analyzed
Paralyzed
Sanctified
Identified
Compartmentalized
Electrified
Prophesied
Polymorphisized
Carbon-neutralized
Anthropomorphized
Leave the feeling alone
Let it get on with
The only job it has
To feel
All feelings
All emotions
All thoughts
Arise, stay a while, and pass away
They are visitors

Dropping by for a cuppa
You don't have to invite them
To stay the weekend.

If I know the truth
It will not be the truth
I am speaking

                                        Be cloud-water
                                        Drift like clouds
                                        Flow like water
                                    Sting like a butterfly
                                        Float like a bee

Without raising a foot
We can still journey
Far

                                    If you find a teacher
                                Who only speaks the truth
                                      Run away quickly

The path to liberation
Is falling into a deep well
Consumed by the *koan* "How do I get free?"

                            With my sitting, I create the path
                        With my silence, I write the discourse
                    With my focus, I silence the five hindrances

You have a perfect life
Every day the same for the first time
Every day the *ying* and the *yang*
The dark and the light
Success, Praise then Rancor, Failure
Wanting more of the former
And less of the latter
Like when you were seven
But with more expensive toys
Just be with what you are experiencing
Be just that

⁂

Kajiwara Hashin wrote
"There is neither
Heaven nor earth -
Only snow falling constantly"
That is all he ever wrote
That is all he ever needed to write
After ten words
He said what he wanted to say
He was done
He left it to lesser lights
Like yours truly
To say too much
If you can't do it
In less than ten words
Better to keep silent
But someone has to write the books
That fill the remainder bins
At Barnes and Noble

⁂

I don't like it
When I get sick
I am in pain
I try to keep sick as just sick
It is bad enough as it is
Why make it worse
By asking "why me?"
Why not me, for goodness' sake

Old friend dying
Shaky, hoarse, thin, weak
Where are you going in such a hurry?

You are whole and complete
Lacking nothing in wisdom, compassion and peace
To know this, awaken the mind
Without resting it on anything
Look at everything, see nothing

Give up all hope
That things will be better -
Things will be just as they are
Even for the king of the world

Lights in my garden
The flowers aren't fooled
They close their petals and sleep

Flashlights in drunkards' hands
Coming home from the pub -
Fireflies in the vale

Read unprinted books
Play unstrung guitars
Revere the Buddha-nature of all things

One summer I drove a truck for an oil company
I was the driver-helper. My partner was the installer
We started at 8:00 a.m. spending all day on the road
Visiting private homes and building sites
Hooking up oil tanks to furnaces.
Our first stop though was at a worker's diner
Where we met up with lots of other
Blue collar guys who worked for themselves
But at breakfast we'd all be part of the brotherhood
Lots of gentle banter between plumbers and electricians
Over who worked harder.
New guys like me took a lot of ribbing
Especially when they found out
I already had two degrees and
Would start a third one soon
They started to call me Einstein
I tried my best to prove them wrong. It wasn't hard. I loved it
The diner was run by a couple from Syria
They had children in school, the oldest, a boy, was my age
They were both very busy.
One day the wife was by herself and looking especially haggard
Someone asked where her husband was
She replied that he died the night before
We were stunned
No one spoke for quite a while
The guys did not shout out for more coffee after that
They got up from the table and served it themselves
They all ate the same thing each morning
So, they simply put the money near the cash and left for work
Nobody wanted to say anything mushy in front of the brotherhood
My partner and I were already late for our first install
I felt queasy when I put the money on the counter
I caught her eye and she smiled
I started to tear up
I hoped none of the guys could see me
She smiled and said, "He was a good man."
I nodded and said "He made good coffee"

I immediately regretted it
"You sound like my eldest," she said "He says stupid things, too."
She had me pegged. She went on.
"But I know he meant to say he loves me"
Yeah. She really had me pegged.

Between heaven and earth
There is no hope -
Only worms in rain puddles

                                        Zen asks you to climb a flower
                                             And water a ladder
                                        Though not at the same time

Coal is black
Under a microscope, coal is not black
Either way, warmed we are

                                        Do not try to be good
                                   Avoid the aspiration to be noble
                              Just be! Leave the modifiers to the eulogists

Behind the veil, another veil
The intellectuals provide a clever answer
To the wrong question and we cheer

                                   To the child a stick may be a gun
                                    To the father it may be a pencil
                                       Both are right and wrong
                                       Zen sees it as just a stick

The world you experience
When you leave the womb is a great shock
We learn strategies to deal with it
We maintain the coping mechanisms
That elicit smiles from family and friends
These become core habits
These become conditionings
And mold us into unique beings
Some of us are fighters
Some of us are pleasers
Some of us hide from confrontation
Some of us repress our anger
Some of us laugh when we are uncomfortable
Some of us cry to get attention
Over time our conditioned responses
Get packaged into a personality
We are funny
Emotional
Meek
Confident
Shy
Bold
Outspoken
Introverted
Obtuse
Anxious
Social
None of this is true
But it feels familiar
Zen helps us to see this conditioned self
And to de-condition our tendencies
Seeing them as just so much flotsam
Floating on the great sea of me
Emptiness is the result
Devoid of all the tainted influences
All the posturings
All the colored glasses we wear
Have clearer lenses now
We see that everything is just that

A monk asked, "How can I escape my bondage?"
The Master asked, "Who is holding you in jail?"

> If you sleep, sleep
> If you eat, eat
> If you walk, walk
> Just don't wobble!

The sage and the ordinary man
Are the same, except the sage
Knows that he knows nothing

> When I was in India, I missed the West
> When I was home, I missed India
> In each country, I lived my passion in misery

Morning doves announce the dawn
Arriving earlier each day
Chirping "Hold the de-caf!"

> Twenty-four years married
> Love more tender and exciting
> Soon my reward: pacemaker

My true home is the journey
From darkness to light
From ignorance to insight
At least, setting myself firmly on the path
Unsure of the destination
But knowing with all my being
What I seek is the seeking
Inertia is not an option
So long ago I set out to find
What I had never lost
To look for what cannot be seen
And listen to what cannot be heard
Like Dylan, I'm on an never-ending tour

❀

There is no practise
You are not preparing
For some future majestic out-of-body experience
You simply sit, stand, walk and lie down
Maintaining a calm abiding
While understanding clearly
Anicca, anatta, dukkha
Uncertainty, no soul, unsatisfactoriness
Doing that, doing nothing, doing non-doing
You are Buddha, an awakened being
This moment IS the real deal, the only deal

❀

Keith Jarrett improvised his famous
Concert in Koln Germany
He is not practicing. He is not playing
Jazz is occurring. Jazz is.
Jazz!
There is no end to practise
And no beginning to playing

A festival of lights
In our backyard
Diwali in the Great White North

                                    Mosquito on my arm
                                    He feeds and buzzes off
                                    Without any thanks. Ouch!

A select group of serious old meditators
Sit very long retreats
Chasing hemorrhoids as much as the truth
I am not so serious
I sit only when I can no longer stand it

                        Home altar, a few Buddhas, icons, avatars
                            So many to venerate, so much bowing
                        Paying respect or simply falling forward?

I rode a donkey once
I didn't know how to ride a donkey
Good that the donkey knew how to carry a me
A lot like Zen, that.

                                        Zen has no goal
                            By the time you are enlightened
                            It's no big deal. You still shit.

Zen is not an empty spirit
It is living life
Doing what needs be done
When it needs be done
Understanding why it needs be done
Without all the fuss and bother
If it had a motto
"Just get on with it"
Would suffice...
In Latin, even better
Sisut proficitis cum eo

✻

Distraction from the angst
Is a band-aid on cancer
Drugs, alcohol, fame, wealth
Are a veneer on the rot
All your worries, thoughts, emotions, judgments
Are ephemeral habits
That usurped their powers
From the unconditioned qualities
Of peace, love and understanding

✻

The sky is impervious
To what bird is flying through
The ocean doesn't give a fig
What fish swims through
The mind need not care
What thought passes through
Sky, ocean, mind
Each with their passing fancies

Even irascible people are doing their best
To survive one more day
With as much joy as possible
Give them a break
And give some even a wider space
If you can't muster up a bit of love
Just say nothing and walk

A half-smile on your face
A twinkle in your eye
Can defuse the ugliest of mindsets

Crows in the Scotch pine
Why so loud?
Be-caws, just be-caws

This being, in this moment
Breathes in
The entire universe

Each and every moment is a lifetime
It is birthed, affirmed and dies
Filled with sufficient life force to birth another moment

Upon the opening of the Buddha-mind
You are everywhere and nowhere
With no direction home
Free to live the unconditioned life
Gate, gate, para sam gate
Gone, gone, gone beyond the distant shore

Trying to get rid of thoughts
Is like asking a deaf neighbor
To turn down his music

For years I looked for peace
I employed techniques, long retreats, yoga
I learned to meditate without meditating
Calmly abiding this body - mind in this moment
Clarity knows no path
Does the sun know how to shine?
Don't be silly, it just shines

❀

Are you meditating or
Thinking you are meditating?
If you can answer this question
You have missed the path.
Meditation is happening
You aren't involved
Nobody is doing nothing
Nothing is being left undone

❀

Much of life is lived
In the in-between
You are often off balance
Out of range
Not quite content
Ill at ease
One unrequited wish away from happiness
Neither here nor there
Always becoming, on the verge
'Twixt birth and death
A visitor to your own life
Which lives a few blocks away

Peace of mind comes not from
Abandoning the ten-thousand things
But from abandoning our attachment
To the ten-thousand things

Waxing or waning
The moon still shines
On the crusted snow

Upon the rolling waves
Of Lake Otty
My heart surfs

Sad is the man
Who is rich
Only in money

Red shirt day
Yellow ribbon, purple socks
Who will we be disrespecting,
When we run out of colors?
Keep your attitude

Keep your actions
As vast as the Sahara
As soft as newly milled flour

Oft-times we have to fall on our face
Before we can succeed
We have to be willing to fail,
To come humbly home, hat in hand,
If we are certain the goal is worthwhile,
That we cannot face another day
Without giving up all that has nurtured us
To take that first tentative step
To the kingdom of redemption
Such was the case 2500 years ago
When Shakyamuni,
Prince Siddhartha
Let go of his wife and only son
And gave up his whole kingdom
To be a homeless Sadhu
The Dhamma is not a hobby
It is not a lifestyle
You have no choice
But to give up your life
To find the truth
Even if it ends in humiliation and rebuke.
To try with all your might
And come up short
Still trumps
Cowering behind the bushes
Pretending...always pretending

❧

Zen can be really boring at times
Providing the opportunity
To see how we blindly react
To an unwanted condition
Along with its wingman
The desire to get rid of it
We learn to calmly abide all the conditions
The way we put up with

The drunk uncle at Christmas dinner.
Remember him?
We listened to him ramble on and on
We didn't say a thing
Eventually he quieted and thanked us for our gift
We hugged him and said we'd see him next year.

How many angels can dance
On the head of a pin?
Great question! Terrible answers

Everything remains a great mystery
When you ponder
Otherwise, just so wonderful

Zen is not something holy
It is not blind faith or divine energy
It is 24/7 effort

Snow-robed mulberry bush
Red cardinals flitting about
Ornithological Conclave

What is mind?
It is the wind
In the painting of a Northern pine

I am now close to the age of my father
When he died
I wish he were here now
He could hold my hand
As we face death together

When you eat, just eat
It is not a spiritual act
Don't worship your food
No need to praise its nourishment
Eat
Don't eat ever so slowly
Uber-masticating every morsel
Displaying how mindful you are
Eat
Don't savor every bite
With your eyes closed in bliss
Eat
Don't use the act of eating
To preach to others
The Zen of eating
Just eat, damn it!

❦

Sometimes you love the practise of Zen
Sometimes you hate it
Sometimes you are focused
Sometimes you are distracted
Sometimes you are alert
Sometimes you are all over the map
Sometimes you are fearful
Sometimes you are brave
Sometimes you are worried
Sometimes you are confident
You think "Now I am getting it!"
Other times, "I am getting nowhere with this!"
Through all this hithering and dithering
The practise of all the Dhamma schools remains
Atapi sampajanna satima
With effort, clear comprehension and mindfulness
See the vicarious mind states and thoughts
For what they are
Understand them
And return to the practise
No foul no harm

There are more incarcerated people
Outside of prisons
Than in them

Letting go of all your identities
Letting go of Buddhism
Letting go of Zen
Now you have nothing
You are home

Tisarana boreal forest monastery
Oasis of calm
Wind in the trees
Blowing the mind to follow

There is no exit
All the doors are locked
Pay attention 'till the bell tolls

In a forest clearing we came upon
A single hole golf course
We waited for someone to shout "Fore"
To which we could reply "One"

In the forest a pine bench
Beckons me to sit
No need to ask twice

Awareness is not enough by itself
If it were, every tightrope walker
Would be giving Dhamma talks
Awareness must be ardent
An effortless effort maintaining focus
Awareness must be accompanied by understanding
That each thought, emotion, judgment, fantasy
Is just that, nothing more
As well it is change itself
In perpetual motion
And therefore, it is unsatisfactory
Unable to make us happy, content or wise
This is the root teaching
Zen exposes us to these laws of nature
This right view must be maintained continuously

❧

Zen does not offer
An extraordinary modifying sacred and holy life
It offers you a mirror
To see your very ordinary life
Just as it is
And just as it really is
Is perfect to realize the truth
Today

❧

Don't get trapped by the chanting,
By the incense, by the rituals,
By the bowing, by the gongs.
All quite mesmerizing
All quite unnecessary
Until they aren't

Log cabin, screened porch
Tattered tartan sofa bed
Loons calls me to dreaming
I thought I already was

Lake Otty's craggy shoreline
Perpendicular pines searching for the sun
As do I after a long winter

Did I have a childhood
So long ago
Today, I have forgotten all my memories

Heavy snow on pine branches
Graze my toque
Hello to you too

Fame and fortune are merely
Laugh tracks and fake applause
With mannequins in the audience

My sons and their mother
Still enjoy the company
Of this worthless poet

Repress nothing
Everything that arises in the mind
Does so to pass away
When we repress it
It remains somewhat buried
In the subconscious
As pure potential
A fifth column
Hiding in the bushes
Ready to attack us
When we let down our guard
We fear this even more
Nothing is as bad
As we thought it might be
Let it be
Let it arise
Let it out into the light
Let it bathe in the sunshine of our
Awareness and equanimity
Calmly abide its prickly persistence
Welcoming it to stay as long as it wants

Do not squander your life
Strive earnestly to awaken
Practice as if tomorrow you die
Each time you find yourself
On a lost trail of idle speculation
Or pondering your future
Snap out of it and ask yourself
"What did I gain from that sojourn?"
The next time
That old familiar song begins
Catch it, watch it and its beguiling nature
Keep it in sight until it passes
Return to the breath

Tree frogs always seem lost
Jumping about, looking for what?
Only the cicada knows, but he never tells

Early morning snowfall
Caught in the glow of a streetlamp
Singular moment of pre-slush glory

Morning run I can see my breath
Frost glazes my beard
Even the thermometer shivers

No one doing nothing
My sons in one hand
The cosmos in the other

Love at first sight
Smiling blue skirt
Honest open face, I fell so hard
I remain bruised to this day

We hold the map upside down
Then we blame it
When we arrive in LA and not NYC

The open heart is boundless
It has no borders
And lots of space
Fear not the arrival
Of negativities
They mean you no harm
They have no intrinsic power
They are just what they are
Their arrival signifies nothing
All smoke no fire
When you are discomforted by them
When you investigate them from different angles
When you want them to disappear
When you dialogue with them
They become energized
They hang around
Like a stray cat that you befriended
With a bowl of milk
Now they are there when you awake
And when you are ready to sleep
They want to be fed
Their cries for attention get louder
Once unwanted guests, they now rule the roost
Stop feeding the cat

❦

Perhaps you have seen the vastness of the cosmos
Maybe you can walk on water
Or see through your ears
What is the point
If tying your shoelaces morphs into an existential crisis?

❦

You aren't trying to end the pain
Because you aren't trying to do anything
You certainly aren't trying to meditate
You aren't trying to remain calm
You aren't trying
Observe the pain
See it as just that
A pain
Not a misfortune
Not an awful catastrophe
Just pain

The Buddha demanded of his monks
Nullius in verba
Take nobody's word for it
Not even his
All truths are *a posteriori*

Drawing fingernail-etchings on frosted windows
My father sits nearby with his coffee
Cold mornings still warm me up

Maybe later, tomorrow perhaps
Putting off freedom until when
You die in chains?

My ignorant parents
Allowed me to make mistakes
I made many and thank them everyday

Moonlight dances on the snow crust
Mica thin reflections
Illuminating the path
For the wan and pithy alike

Basho, master of poetry
Wrote of mundane things
As if they were really nothing
Isn't that something

I want to live in the country
With deer and foxes as neighbors
Easy nights on porches with screen doors
Beat up Ford pickup in the lane
I want to live like that
Maybe, I just think I want to live like that
At least, I think I like thinking I want to live like that

Zen is hard
Because we look at things
As we have been conditioned to look at them
We are in our comfort zone doing so
We think Zen makes us uncomfortable
We blame the teachers.
The rituals, the cushions, the chanting, the food,
The constant noise in the constant silence
Zen is hard enough
But our conditioned mind makes it even more so
We hope to do an end run around our discomfort
There is no beltway around its center
All paths lead though the core

There is only the experience
Pure and simple
Each moment is experienced
Pay attention. Pay attention
Conditioned mind adds
Commentary, judgment, comparison,
Spices it with emotion and memory
Pay attention to that too
It is all experience
Experience is just that

A spindled table top cracked
In need of a coat of stain
Grandad won it in a race
Too slow now to win another

Old birdhouse fifty years you've been open
Where are your tenants?
Retired in Florida, I suppose

For many years I walked the path
To return here with home, wife and children
My life, a wonderful mistake!
Ah, a cup of tea

I reject your metaverse
I abhor the omniverse
I cherish life as it is
Harsh honest beauty
I do not need Oculus Rift
To see the minnows in the pond

On the city bus
Gazing, hands in my lap
I re-discover the city of my youth

I feel ill, time to go
Firewood piled high
A waste of energy

A man stepped on a thorn
Ouch!
His friend picked up the thorn,
Looked at it,
No suffering
The suffering is not in the thorn
The thorn can't hurt me
If I leave it be
The suffering comes when we consistently step
On the bright shiny thorns

Do not regret what has passed
The days we thought would never end
Wine, roses and camaraderie
We laughed like the gladiators of old
Living on the high,
On the far out, man
Without this forsaken revelry
The days and nights of experience
The present monastic forbearance
The days of innocence
Could not be realized
Real wisdom, real insight
Letting go of the bright lights
And the 10,000 shiny things
Happy now with
The mundane, the old, the simple
Deeply content with the daily miracles
Of the small things

What is tragic is not the suffering
Misery, dissatisfaction, and pain
Comes to us all, over time
What is tragic is identifying
With the suffering
It is mine. I am a sufferer
I am the victim here
And so, you will be
Until the end of your days

I like my routines
Except when they upset my habits
Or conflict with my rituals

Picking *kosari*
Hiding in plain sight
A sun-dappled sleep in the long grass

Autumn -
The trees, and even
The clouds change mind

On Cheju's isle
Yellow fields of rapeseed
Enclosed by volcanic lava rock walls
Aftermath of Mount Halla's mighty eruption -
I run with hand over head

I like trees
With scars and broken branches
Bent seeking the sun
Each a story, some true, some just real
All worth a listen

Mighty monsoon thunder
Propelled me out of bed -
Where have the six directions (including up and down) gone?

My mother used to say
"It's always something"
She was paraphrasing
The Buddha's First Noble Truth
And Michael Stipe
"Everybody hurts"
Everybody

***

Do not be afraid of falling off the wagon
Blind indoctrination is the real problem not the stumble
Real wisdom emerges in the mud
Falling flat on our face
Failing again and again
One mistake after another
Then like Saul on the road to Damascus
We see
We profoundly know
No more doubts or fears
Now, this here is the Path

***

Appreciate the life with which you have been blessed
Birth is an extremely rare opportunity
To do the stuff of a human being
Wake up to your birthright
All those born will eventually die
Sooner or later
All those born will experience
Honor and shame
Success and failure
Gain and loss
Pleasure and pain
At different times
In different degrees

Suffering begins when we
Judge others to have more attainments
Based only on outward appearances
This is not so
Everybody hurts

Summer cottage coffee
Loons calling across the lake
Calm sky-reflecting water
An Eden without forsaken fruit

Soon I'll buy a new car
Then I'll purchase a turntable
Shopping for more shiny bright things
In the tomorrow aisle

When the 10,000 things are seen
They are shiny and bright
When the Path is explained
It is flavorless and plain
And yet those who chose the Path
Never speak of regret

You only find yourself
When you forget yourself

Anxiety is the underhanded thief of childhood
Burdened by too many choices and options
Too early in life

I had nothing to do today
I got so busy sitting
I ended up with no time to do nothing

Because I know so much
I am a stupid father
I have opinions about everything my sons do
They do not think things through
They make bad choices
I am on top of it
My own father worked two jobs
He had little education
After I turned fifteen
He left me alone
To make mistakes
And I sure did
And then he would forgive me
And smile as if to say
"You'll figure it out"
And I did

The Buddha was a worthless fellow
An absentee father, he had no job
Fortunately, making a living
Though an economic necessity
Is not an existential one

Chuang Tzu said
"There is nothing that is not so
Nothing that it is not acceptable"
If it can be thought
It is part of the Tao
Hence it requires acceptance
Not judgment
Though everything is within human nature
And within nature
This does not mean

We cannot do better
Monks have 227 precepts
Guidelines they are asked to follow
To make living in a community
Better, easier and more peaceful for all

The louder your parade
The more likely
Rain will fall on it

What is life all about?
Is a ridiculous question -
The answer, even more so

Geckos drop from the ceiling
On to my mosquito net
My protection, their trampoline

Under the maple tree
There are no strangers

Do you envy
The skaters on the frozen canal
Winter moon?

My love and I held hands
On a mid-stream rock
We spoke in silent whispers
And made promises we still keep

In everyone's life
No matter their station
Comes opportunities often unannounced
To be kind
You don't have to love
You don't have to even like
They might be homeless and drug addicted
And asking for some spare change
Even without making a donation
You can be kind
You can smile
Kindness imbues your life
With sublime sunshine
It softens your rage
It temporarily pardons your shortcomings
If you elicit a smile in return
From a crying child,
From a stranger
From a lonely senior
You have done a good deed
In time, also unannounced,
You will be rewarded
Ten-fold

We chant
Sanditthiko, akaliko, ehi passiko,
Paccatam veritabho vinnuhi
The Dhamma is
Here and now, timeless, turning towards the truth,
Leading inwards, known only through direct experience
What more could you ask for?

All are visited by many stupid and embarrassing thoughts
Trying to repress, negate or deny them
Grants them more power than they deserve
They're just thoughts, mind blips, neuro-burps
All smoke and no fire
Leave them be
Our hearts are very large
Set these thoughts over there, in the corner,
Comfortable but out of the way
Not worth your admonishment

Love everybody
Except for the people who complain a lot
And all the haters. What's with them?

                              Our life, warts and all,
                                Is there all the time
                          Ready to be experienced anew
                        Again and again for the first time

Night frost
Morning flour-dusted grass
Crocuses with ear muffs

                                          Drought
                            Grass withers, weeds spread
                      Buddha-natures simply unfolding

Do not cling to simplicity and emptiness
Nor fear too many possessions
The meaning is self-evident
Even to talk about it
Is to say water is wet

                                    The two are one
                                    The one are two
                                 One of these is false
                                Though both are true

Sing the song of less
The one note dirge
Of poverty and few
Sing the praises of
The miracles of small things
The overlooked and underwhelmed

My mother would make
A pot of tea
Whenever I visited
The tea was very strong
She used a lot of tea leaves
Which she would read afterwards
She was a bit of a mystic
When she was younger
She visited a fortune teller
Who told her three men
Would ask to marry her
And she would accept the third
The war in Europe was in its final days
And within a few weeks
Two men asked her to marry them
She said they were too tall and handsome
She waited a few more months
When the third man
My not tall not handsome father returned
And popped the question.
She accepted
He made her laugh.
And he was a gentle man
In my cup my mother
Always saw me walking with a young child
I saw a monk walking with a begging bowl
In a way we were both right
I guess we both saw what we wanted to see

We tilt our spears at windmills
Declaring ourselves knights in armor
Standing before our mirror, posturing always

Canada geese flocking north
Shoots breaking through earth -
Fear of the white wind remains

Spring
Early morning bird-song
Dew worms on parade

What is, is *ki*
Not mind inside
Not God outside
Inside, outside: one
Only no opinions are true

Yung Chia tells us
Not to seek the truth
Nor cut off delusions
Stop trying so hard. Live

Fresh-baked bread
Doesn' t discriminate
Wafting to nostrils of prince and beggar

Wisdom cannot come
From the tip of a pencil
Nor from lectures and talks
TED's or other's
It comes from the heart
Of innocence and experience
A life lived close to death
Without surrender to lucre or fame
Truth in this moment
Is in front of you
See it now!
With closed eyes
And open heart

Poetry is not an art
It is a compulsion,
An itching
An eruption of thought-provoking lava
That explodes from the pen
Producing from time to time
A bastard child
Bright beyond his years
Exceeding expectations
It matters not how long
The child will live
But only that
In the moment it lived
Shouting with the ferocity of Bukowski
And the brevity of Basho
The poet claims no ownership
Nor even authorship
More conduit than creator
More thief than poet
More illusionist than writer
More persistent than successful
He will continue putting pen-to-paper
Until he gets it write

Fallen leaves in the spring
Hidden under shadowed snow
Somehow still dead

Clapping hands
The waiter brings tea
Dogs bark
Birds fly up
On the river of *samsara*

We think it is easy, it is not
We think it is hard, it is not
Judging it to be thus and so
Unnecessary distractions

Even celestial stars break up
As do the Hollywood variety
Both hiding behind non-disclosure agreements

The faster, the slower
The more you strive
The further away it gets

Buds swell in the spring
Without worry or hurry
Each day an eternity
Without a moment to lose

The thing is not
What we suppose it to be
Nor is it different from what we see
It simply is
Devoid of all its implications
More a product of mind
A seen-thing
A heard-thing
A felt-thing
A smelt-thing
A tasted-thing
A thought thing
The conditioned mind
Adds memory and reaction and habit and like and dislike
The unconditioned mind
The Buddha-mind
Sees the thing just as it is

There is path and there is non-path
Path is straight and true
Non-path is crooked and problematic:
Over-grieving inevitable sorrows
Over-attaching to fleeting joys
Regarding as permanent
What is transitory
Always looking for the silver lining
Wanting things to be non-existent
Wanting things that are impossible
Conditioning the mind in the process
To continue in the crooked way
Falsely thinking there can be
No other way
This is the great blindness
That the Buddha diagnosed

A thing is one thing, and all things
Sameness and difference, two things yet one
Ice, water, steam, heaven

The second law of thermodynamics
Wind in summer-long grass
Quivering

Water buffalo mind
Rain, heat, night, day
Keep the buff close

Healthy as a horse
Outliving them all
You won the race, how lonely

The space/time continuum shudders
In the wake of Buddha-mind
Blake: one thought fills immensity

Multi-colored tulips
The intrepid gardener
Withdraws his scissors

Nature abounds we say when
Water flows, clouds drift,
Buds open, leaves fall,
Seasons come and go
Years pass
Everything in nature is just that
Hold on to nothing
Behold, your hands are full

Be at home
In the cafe and the temple
Dine with paupers and oligarchs
Walk on paved streets and forest paths
Seek neither company nor solitude
Welcome all and sundry to home
Love your life and do not fear death
Attach to nothing
Even to non-attachment

In Igatpuri we woke at four a.m.
To sit a few hours
In the meditation sala
Leaving for breakfast at daybreak
The sunrise breathing in
The silence of our minds
The silence of our steps
As we rounded the corner
We heard the pleas of the *chai wallas*
At the railroad station down the hill
I bowed my head in silent prayer
"Please, this morning,
Idlis with coconut chutney"

The heart is always whole
As the moon is always full
Except when my son gets in the way

                                        This moment, now
                                        Exists and non-exists
                                        Known only in its passing
                                        Doing a Higgs-Boson

No cow, no moo
No moo, no cow
To cow is to moo
To moo is to cow
Children have it right-
They call it a moo-cow

                                        By not going, we arrive
                                        By not speaking, we teach
                                        By not eating, we are full
                                        By not reading, we understand

Follow the teacher who collects not devotees
Who speaks in sentences without words
Understanding is a flash of lightning
Gone before it crackled
We don't know what it is
Because it is a "What was that?!"

                                        Be content with too much or too little
                                        Excess or famine
                                        What's the difference to a free man?

Once a thing is named
Other is created
Streams, rivers, brooks, seas, bays, oceans
This is one, those are others
In the end
All are water

The fates and furies
Can drive us off course
Set us back
Upset our dreams
Destroy what gains we have made
This is a pessimistic view
Based on false assumptions
We charted a course
Never having studied navigation or meteorology
We carved it in stone
Now we find ourselves
Off the coast of Tasmania
Heading south

You do battle with your conditioning
It revolts under calm abiding
It reacts with boredom, pain, hope, fear
It craves excitement, pleasure, success, confidence
Face this barrage with stillness,
Maintain your awareness,
Keep your equanimity
Grow in understanding
That the impediments to success are worthy adversaries
Knowing that the battle demands an effortless effort
Is the harbinger of success

Hecato decreed
Cease to hope and you
Will never be afraid again

So many questions, doubts and fears!
Trust in the path and your own heart
You want to debate, I want to sleep

The Buddha lived 2,500 years ago
He is also a clay statue in my room
Is no thing devoid of Buddha-nature?

Zen is the lighting of the fire,
Brewing the tea and setting the table -
Don't let my words spoil elevensies

Round and round the world I went
To finally settle down with my wife
In the place I was raised
Forty years I played the Circle game

Sit while standing
Sit while lying down
Even sit while in a wheelchair
Full lotus, always

Life is no big deal
It is simply what we do
With what we have
It is, however, the only deal in town
Every life is perfect
No life is better or worse
Than any other
In the same way that
Every event, reaction, thing
Every touch, smell, taste, sight, noise or thought
Is an opportunity for insight
Into the human condition
And as our understanding and wisdom deepen
As we befriend the *yin* and *yang*
Understanding everything is just that
Then life moves along
At its own pace
As do we, doing the stuff of human beings

❦

"How are you?" I am asked many times a day
My standard reply is "I'm fine"
But if I thought about it
As a genuine question
Rather than a greeting
I would reply
"About how you would expect for a human being in my situation"

❦

I hope I expire
Before I fully mature
I don't mind looking like
A rabid goat
As long as I maintain
My ten-year-old heart

It keeps me giggling
Giving raspberries
And breaking wind
In the Church of the
Sanctimonious Prudes

Buddha
Not a God, not a saint
Simply a-wake

Evensong
When we gather at the river
The frogs look heavenward

Even loons raise waves
When there is no wind -
Canoes are unstable enough as it is

Moonlit shadows of scraggly branches
That was really what it was
The skeleton that I saw

Why must
I stretch my arms
To touch the sky?

When I am ill
The universe has a fever
When I recover, it continues to expand

"Good surf today," or
"Poor surf today," they say.
Not really. The ocean is just doing ocean.
It does not get caught up
In all the meteorological blather.
And when you are the ocean everything else
Is just so much blather.

The ocean is always the ocean.
Sometimes there are a lot of waves.
"The ocean is angry today," they say.
No, it is not.
Other times many icebergs are seen.
"The ocean is dangerous today," they say.
No, it is not.
And at all times there are ships.
"The ocean is crowded," they say.
No, it is not.
What occurs on the surface of the ocean
Does not phase the ocean.
It continues oceaning 24/7.
Tides come in, tides go out.
Our mind is like this.
Its capacity is oceanic
More storage capacity
Than an Amazon warehouse
Generating googles of compassion,
Empathy, love and humility.
It too has lots of surface blather,
Blind reactions and emotional responses
So, we must learn from the ocean
To not react to the surface blather
To not get caught up with
The odd super-tanker
That floats across the mind's surface

Spilling its oil hither-nither
And tooting its horn
Demanding the icebergs and islands
Get out of the way.

All pairs of opposites
Are created by conditioned mind
Seeing one as two - the tap-root of suffering

Leaves fall in Autumn
Buds form in the Spring
This is their nature
It cannot be hurried or halted

The perfected mind
Beyond duality
Easily passes through
The key hole of the universe

Neighbor's dogs greet me every morning
I reply excitedly and the conversation ensues
All of us surprised that I speak bark

Emptiness
Full of nothing
Tune in, turn on the unconditioned

Faces on the Metro
Gazing at other faces
Seeing reflections of themselves, perhaps

I studied philosophy
To get an answer to the big question
"What is life all about?"
I left school with more questions
Than when I began,
Questions like
"How does logical positivism
Make me happier?"
I learned more about my mind
From Dostoevsky and Alexander Portnoy
Than Logic and Semantics
Philosophy allowed me to
Reference Heidegger and Kant
Impressing undergraduates
With my veritas, my intellect and my pipe smoke
My big question now is
"Where is my mind as I rake my leaves?"
Is it just here now or has it been hijacked
By old habitual thought patterns
So, I am no longer raking leaves
But lollygagging with an old lover
On a fall day?
"Am I present?"
The really big question.

※

"Every day" is a meaningless expression
Literally, it means what it says
But in essence,
It conjures connotations in the mind
Of a life sentence in solitary
You have to set your mind to tackling
A difficult undertaking
For one day
Just one day of silent meditation
There, that wasn't so bad, was it?

Not many people can meditate for thirty days
But most can handle a one-day retreat.
Thirty one-day retreats
Even that is too much?
How about a one-hour retreat?
Eight one-hour retreats a day

Across the swamp, stitcher lady bathes
She waves hello and smiles
She thinks I am Buddha -
Tomorrow, I will bring her a mirror

Mud hut on the Gangetic Plain
Cool in day, warm at night
Geckos bouncing on my head

Everything is just that, this we call truth
It has never been hidden
Here! There! All around!

The path is not difficult
Simply don't
Choose or reject

In my dreams, I am very young
I wake and wonder
When a young boy dreams
Is he my age?

High winds, minus thirty tonight,
Nature's revenge for the festival?
Even the ice sculptures shiver

I left Ubon by bus
Not sure at all
Where I was being taken
I spoke little Thai
The *maeban* on the bus
Spoke no English
The jungle thickened
My anxiety intensified
After some time
The driver called me to the front
Opened the door
And bid me *"sawasdee krab"*
I stood alone in the jungle
And watched the bus disappear
I saw a low white stone wall
And followed it for a while
Finally, a gate
Fortunately, open
I walked through it
Thinking it must lead somewhere
It was soon after that
I heard a temple gong
I breathed a sigh of relief
Soon the Dhamma Sala
Of Wat Pa Nana Chat
Came into view.
My anxiety drained away
All that tension
All that doubt
All that fear
All of it my own creation

Matheran tribal area Saturday market
Young girls dressed in their finery
Shopping for lentils and husbands

How many angels on the head of a pin?
Noumena? Phenomena? Kant? Hegel?
"Nonsense" says the moon this starry night

Is it okay to want less?
Is it okay to crave anonymity?
Craving is craving - rich, famous just be that

Young aspen, brown frozen leaves
Tinkling in the winter wind
Let go, my dears, let go

Smell of Autumn
Warm sweater and toque
Logs in the fireplace - waiting
I can hear the Snow Gods stirring

Above Igatpuri train station
I sleep-dream to the sounds
Of whistles, engines, touts and *chai walla*s - heaven

Behind and below Dhammagiri's hill
There was a tribal farming village
I lived in a one room *kuti*
With a small porch
From which I could see
The whole valley
Deeded to the tribals
I would sit on my porch
As the farmers brought
The cattle back from their fields
For milking
They encouraged their return
With cries and singing
In Marathi
I detected no hurry
With the corralling
Neither with the farmer
Nor the cattle
It was a scene that had not changed
Over the centuries
Every day saw the same procession
The same song-like exhortations
The same lowing from the cattle
The farmers, their cattle,
Their dependents and the land they worked
Were tethered together
Joined at the hip
None able to live without the other
So entwined were their lives
There was no sense of one and other
All were realizing their true nature
Everything was just that
Beings being beings

The death knell for wisdom
Is the proclamation
"Ain't I somethin?"

You don't need to be incarcerated
To be a prisoner

Windy autumn day
On empty baseball fields and silent streets
I search for the kites of my youth

Bathe in the forest
Yielding all your pain
To the towering pines

Excessive humility
Is excessive pride
I know
I was the first on my block to lose my ego!

You
Me
Whee!

For a while I lived at a yoga ashram
In rural Pennsylvania
The guru was an ex-Indian Air Force pilot
Who emigrated to America
And became a yoga teacher
This was the era of Baba Ram Dass
Hippie LSD Harvard professor
Who spoke of the love and divine power
Of Neem Karoli Baba his guru
It was the time of Mahara-ji,
A chubby fifteen-year-old boy
Filled the Astrodome
Waiting for World peace
Back in Pennsylvania
The simple yoga teacher
Was encouraged by his students
To be a real teacher,
A guru
He agreed
He took to wearing brocaded robes
He grew his hair
And gave videotaped Darshans
He was worshipped
He gave cryptic answers
That implied astral projection
It was the dawning of the age of Aquarius
His main *sidi* was *shakti pat*
The transmission of divine grace
Two hundred disciples
Reacted to shafts of energy
With cries of joy and screaming
It was a form of mass hypnosis
Like found at a Beatles' concert
I was not comfortable with this
External force of power
Only those who had fully surrendered to the Guru
Could really feel its purifying powers

That left me, gladly, out in the cold
Years later he was charged with sexual impropriety
And the yoga ashram became a health spa
For the wealthy elite
Once again, I was gladly out in the cold

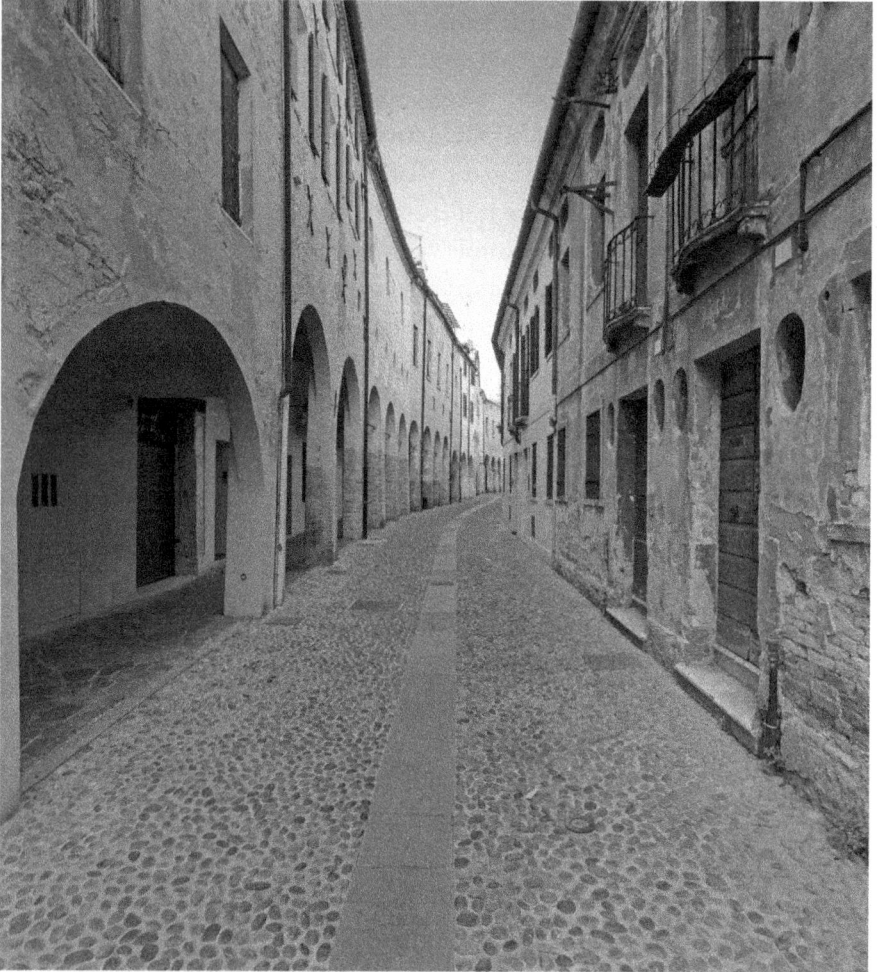

You can't be pro
Without being anti
We are all prejudiced. All.

Rubbing a brick all day won't make it a mirror
Just sitting all day won't make you enlightened -
Remember, even chickens sit

This and that
Here and there
You and me
Are one
Without this, there can be no that
Without here, there can be no there
Without me, there can be no you

The path is said to be easy. It is not
Others say the path is hard. It is not
The path is the path
Tautological perfection

Light contains a spectrum
Of all the possible colors
By itself, colorless
We too contain multitudes
By myself, emptiness

Emptiness is just as it is
No duality, no separation, no identity
Everything, is just that
Zen, all-powerful Hoover

It is not lethargic inertia
It is an active stillness
It is engaged non-engagement
There can be no activity
Without stillness
And no stillness
Without activity

❦

Avoiding conflict is not Path
Nor is reveling in conflict
Living in duality
Where there is this and there is that
Conflict is bound to ensue

❦

I lose my glasses all the time
I can only find my glasses
After I have found my glasses
My only solution
Is to stop looking for my glasses
Until I find them
At which time, I didn't lose my glasses at all
Because I wasn't looking for them
And they were right where I left them
They are usually on my nose anyway

❦

When I whistle, my dog comes
When the kettle whistles, I come
When the factory whistles, the workers go home
When the sirens whistle, people seek shelter
When I get a needle, I whistle
But my dog doesn't come

Whistling is a complex issue
We need to get to the bottom of this
Leveraging strategic strategies
Drilling down to find the secret sauce
We need to keep on top of things
And get them under control
If we all get behind this issue
We can get ahead of the curve

The swallows make nests
In the eaves of palaces
And barns

                                        The sun glistens
                                        On the morning dew
                                        Morning coffee needs dark glasses

Apple blossoms
Cover my trail
I walk on *anicca*

                                        The gem of wisdom
                                        Lies hidden in a mountain
                                        Only one who cannot climb
                                        Finds it

The Zen answer
Is never "I don't know"
But "I have no-idea"

                                        There comes a time
                                        When Zen finally is understood
                                        Even if it still doesn't make sense

If you don't understand
At least understand
That you don't understand
Then there is nothing
That you don't understand

❦

You are not the owner
Of your thoughts
They arise naturally and constantly
From the primordial ether
Of the mind
Cognizing
Recognizing
Feeling
Reacting
Digging deeper and deeper gullies
For ensuing rains-thoughts to fill
Show me the suffering
Of generations past
Where is it now?
Why hold on to it?
Recreating
Reliving
Reviving
Returning
Rekindling
As if it happened
Only moments ago
Without your constant visitations
The suffering
Calms,
Perspective
Forgiveness
Understanding
Arise.

Does my breath not know
A war is going on?
Still, it comes in and goes out
Does it not read the news?

Meditate until you see
Meditation is unnecessary
Then keep on meditating

The teaching of Zen is wordless
Giving a flower, sharing a smile
You cannot know what it is
Because it is not a what

Suffering occurs
When we divide the universe into two
Judging one-half, better

Tell a lie often enough
It becomes true -
All truth was once a lie

Writing about Zen
Is like explaining Autumn
To a maple tree

I was about ten years old
My father and I were fishing at dusk
We were in a punt
That had a small leak
And a wonky outboard engine
It started to get dark
The wind picked up and it poured rain
The engine of course conked out
My dad started rowing
I grabbed a rusty tin can
And started bailing
We were going into the wind
Waves were pushing us back
Almost as fast as we moved forward
My father turned around
To see if we were getting any closer to the shore
"What's that?" My father asked me
I looked up from my bailing
He was right something off in the distance
That looked like a light
As we focused our eyes in that direction,
Easing off our rowing and bailing
Another light appeared, then another
The cottages on the shore!
We shouted with joy
We doubled our efforts
I took over the rowing and father, the bailing
This time it was me who spotted something
That seemed to be moving
And coming closer to us
Another shout of joy erupted
"Ahoy," we yelled
We returned to rowing and bailing
We kept up that torrid pace
Until a large motorboat pulled up and threw us a line
They had seen us out fishing earlier
And when we hadn't returned after the storm hit

They set out on a rescue mission
We were exhausted and soaked to the bone
As we stood on the beach and caught our breath
We couldn't help but notice the power lines were down
The cottages had no lights

When the carved sculpture
Starts his song
The stone statues begin to dance

                              "How will I know
                        Which monk is enlightened?"
                        "Bring a melon," was the reply
                              "He loves melons"

Everyday mind
Sits quietly and smiles
Amid contradictions

                        Some Zen monks use *koans*
                              For we householders
                        Life with family is our *koan*

Nisargadatta was clear
"No remedy but one
The search for remedies must cease"

                        Sarnath, Dhammacakkappavattana
                              Turning of the wheel
                              I walk in the Deer Park
                              Along my cottage road

I well remember the first time I meditated
By then drugs and alcohol had fallen away
I had started doing yoga
I was a runner
And a vegetarian
I visited a Sri Chinmoy center
For some instruction
The guru was a runner and a vegetarian
That first night they gave me a sitting cushion
I stared at a candle
Then I closed my eyes
I saw the candle
That was enough
I felt at peace for a second or two
And "knew this"
was important
Without really knowing
What "knowing" I knew
Nor what "this" was that I knew
I felt in every fiber of my being
That I had started on a path
I would continue come hell or high water
I have meditated every day since. Every. Day.
The Path changed my life in every way possible
All for the better
This all started with a hunch
A burning itch I couldn't scratch
An intuition
A pure intuition
Free from ulterior motives
I trusted that intuition
With hindsight I believe
Intuition cannot arise
From a morass of drugs and alcohol
My first teacher Roshi Philip Kapleau
A successful businessman in NYC
Heard a few talks by D.T. Suzuki back in the fifties

The spark was ignited
He quit his job, sold everything he had
Moved to a Zen Temple in Japan
Becoming the first American to be ordained.
You know when you know

To awaken to pure awareness
Is to realize "I" am nothing -
Oh, as well as everything

Life, death
All an illusion
And yet...and yet

When autumn winds blow
Even the scarecrow
Shivers

I have walked
In Korea and Canada -
The moon remains far

We humans are real
Why look for reality
Outside ourselves?

Awakening is sudden
After decades of
Striving

Zen is simply paying attention to pain
Understanding that pain is just that
An uncomfortable feeling
No, not uncomfortable
Just a feeling
No, not even a feeling
Just sensations on the body/mind
Free of intention, valuation, judgment
Leave it alone
Welcome it even
Stay with it
Understand it
It does not mean to hurt you
It doesn't want you to suffer
It is just that
Then a space opens up around the pain
Allowing you to honestly face,
With a dusting of equanimity,
All which you have resisted or fled from for years
Pain of a sort remains
The existential pain of
Birth
Sickness
Old age
Death
Separation from those we love
Nothing we can do about certain pains
But we need not suffer

So many questions
You already know the answer
You only wish you didn't
Now, drink your tea

A *koan* for the rest of us:
What is the sound
Of one family kvetching?

I am with me
Wherever I go
Palace or prison
Baggage and all

It never always gets worse
Calm down
This will not last forever

St. Augustine decreed
"If you had not already found me,
You would not be seeking me."
If you didn't already possess Buddha-mind
You wouldn't be seeking Buddha-mind

Every breath must be earnest and honest
Only then can you stay still
Sitting in the fire

Whether you admit it or not
Deep in every being
Is the desire to find God
In your own way you will seek him out
I was very devout as a child
I found God
In the holy trinity
Church, family and hockey
At seventeen I began
To look for different answers
To different questions
Along with millions of others in my cohort
A few found the answer in God, in a guru, in Garcia
Many others in a reasonable facsimile thereof
With drugs, with communal living,
With radical politics, with Eastern mystics
Later generations turned the hippie trip
On its head worshiping at the altar
Of the almighty dollar
Investment banking, early retirement,
Financial independence.
The millennials took a giant step leftwards
Prostrating themselves before
Another holy trinity
Jobs, Zuckerberg and Musk
Praising hi-tech, Google,
The internet of equity, inclusivity and diversity
Virtual reality, on-line learning
You may not agree with the entire spectrum of Gods
But one will resonate with you
Listen carefully and critically

There is only one thing worse
Than lacking goodness
That is, believing you are good

Everything is just that
In Zen, just that, unconditionally
Is your Buddha-nature

The scent of campfire
Halos the moon -
Silent conversation as we sit around
Watching smoky swirls of Rothkos

No samanera
Rakes the leaves
At daybreak

Zen is the life
Of the plumber and the plutocrat
Of the ecclesiast and the atheist
At the end of the day
All eat their rice and wash their bowl

Words can only express words
The word "match" cannot start a fire
Come, I'm hungry. Let's eat the menu!

When in Mumbai I would stay
At the Lawrence Hotel
On Rope Walk Lane
It was more than a hotel for me
It was my home
As it was with
Countless other Dharma Bums
Only six rooms
You had to book your bed early
Al who owned the hotel and
Lived upstairs with his wife and son
Knew all of us
And would do his best to
Place us in a room with a friend
Not that hard of a job
Since we were all friends anyway
Mornings were the best
We were close to the Ocean
So, it was cool and breezy
Breakfast arrived around 8:00 a.m.
Oatmeal, a bun
And unlimited pots of tea
We generally ate with our doors open
Better to politely accost anyone who had ventured out earlier
To buy a papaya to ask if they wanted
To join us for breakfast
Everyone knew you only
Buy the largest papaya available
Dharma Bums have been known to smell a fresh papaya
From a hotel blocks away
There were a couple of touts hanging around
Who would buy train tickets for us
To save us standing in line for hours
We would give them a pile of rupees
And our passport
And not give it another thought
Al vouched for their honesty

And everyone vouched for Al
Being in the company of like-minded people
Was like being back home
With the best family
You never had

We are not engaged in mysticism
We seek not the spiritual or the mystical
Dhamma and everyday life are not two

At first there is wonder
When we realize the unity of all things
Roshi Joko called it ordinary wonder

Do you accept my teaching?
Not all, maybe half
Good, now you are being true to my teaching

Life by itself is perfect
You need not a mission or a calling -
A chicken with a broken wing, still lays

Trying to find Shangri La?
You are standing on it
Hakuin: This earth is the Pure Lotus Land

Nisargadatta: When the mind is quiet
It withdraws from experience and the one who experiences
Leaving only pure awareness

When I was ten years old
My mother would read me passages
From "The Importance of Living"
By Lin Yutang
This was my first exposure
To philosophy in general
And specifically, to Confucianism and Taoism
It was this treatise
That set the stage for my later studies
And imbued within me
An admiration of things Oriental
To paraphrase the title of this book
The most important aspect of my life
At that time was to have fun
I was given freedom to do so
No strings attached
Short of requiring hospitalization
But I admit to feeling some trepidation
Of what was in store for me
As I watched those older than me
Trudge off to work
They didn't seem to laugh
Pieces of paper, kept in files
Seemed very important to them
Lin Yutang painted an alternative scenario
Of philosophers who dream yes,
But with one eye open
They viewed life with love and irony
Intellectual cynicism mixed with kindly tolerance
He formulated life from the Chinese perspective
As reality + dreams + humor = wisdom
To a ten-year old
Wary of scowling faces sitting on buses
This seemed to be the way to live
Sixty-five years later
I still think so.
My mother didn't realize what she started

Whatever impediments are uncovered
In Zen are robbed of their power to harm
When we remain aware

There is nothing to gain from Zen
There is really no reason to do it
Just sit through every mood
Letting doubt, boredom, futility be

Ladybug, ladybug
I found you this February morn
Dead, sleeping or premature *kensho*?

Does the wind
Propel the sailboat
Or do the sails
Pull the wind?

Are there hidden trails
In the sky,
Winter moon?

Hokku
Emptiness of all things -
Even my cup brimming with tea

The nearest city to my *kuti* was Nasik
One of the seven holy cities
Situated at the confluence of five rivers
I could get there by bus or taxi
Either way I was putting my life at risk
Indian highways are single lane
Trucks and buses travel at light speed
Down the center of the road
They honk their horn
Informing the opposing vehicle that
They are coming their way
At the last moment both veer slightly
Towards their respective shoulders
Missing each other by inches before
Regaining their composure.
Accidents invariably occur when
One of the vehicles is a truck
Stacked higher than the law allows.
When this truck veers quickly
The load may shift
And keep shifting even after
The truck moves back to center
The load takes the driver
And the truck to which he is attached
Onto the shoulder and beyond
Sometimes to the great beyond
If I remained *compos mentis*
I could walk from the bus station
To the ghats
Steps built millennia ago
Going down to the river
Going back in time
2,500 years ago at least
When you emerge
The scene before you
Reflects the time of the Buddha
Women wash clothes,

Cows roam freely
Elephants are washed by their mahouts
Surrounded by a large market selling all manner of goods
As it has done on this spot since before time
I order a *chai* and sit and breathe in eons

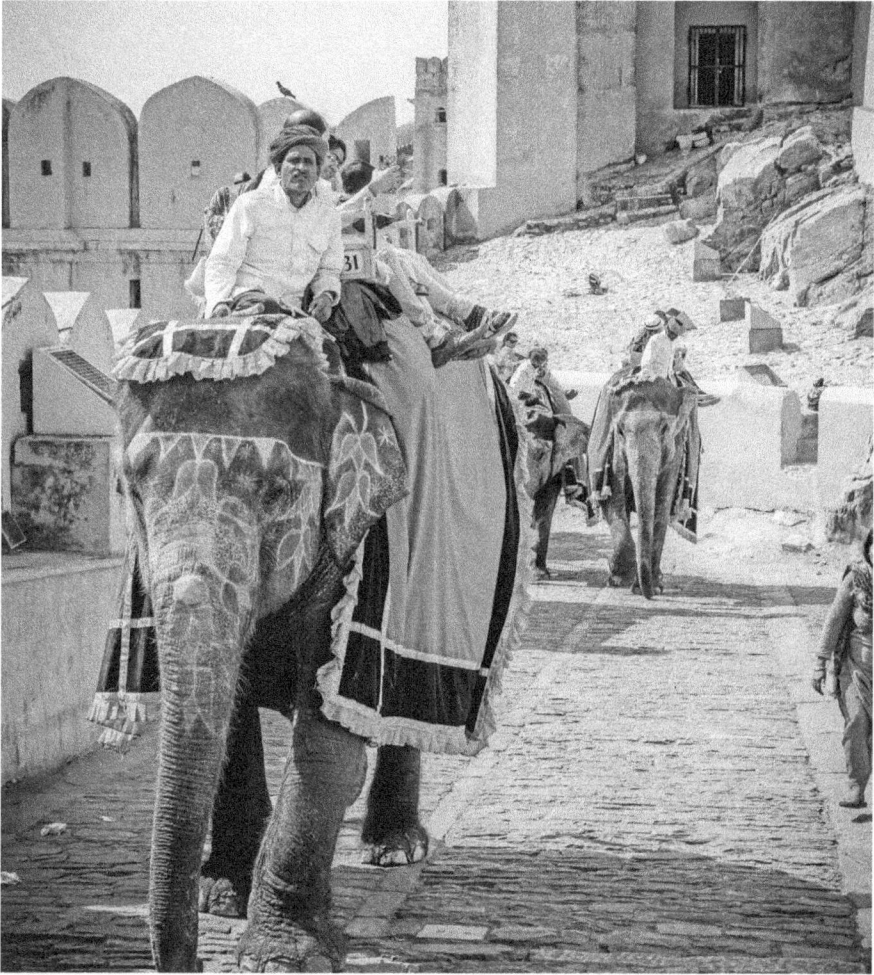

A rainbow of kayaks
In perfect color spectrum order -
Marvelling, I sit on the old cedar dock

After a dream
Of summer days at the lake
How cold the floor

I sneeze
Blue Heron elegantly lifts off -
"Enough with your sniffling"

A cord of logs
Waiting in the sun
To dry then to ash

Lagom
Even this little
Is enough

Finding a four-leaf clover
At eight years of age
I forget what I wished for
But I'm glad it didn't come true

In my teens when I pondered
A future career
I eliminated all the usual suspects
Doctor, lawyer, accountant
Until I stared straight at only one option
That resonated with me
Shepherd
From church I heard lots of stories about shepherds
They were watching their flocks by night
Probably collecting overtime,
As Jesus' birth star passed overhead
David himself, writer of Psalms
Had a day job as a shepherd
I had never read of an evil shepherd
That Christ had banished to the jungle
Denying the obvious reality
That I lived in a housing project
In the urban core of a large city
I set my heart on shepherding
I liked the idea
Of being responsible for the well-being and safety
Of my flock
I could sit in the shade of a large tree
Reading a book or writing my own psalms
While the sheep frolicked
An activity I could relate to
No one telling me what to do
There seemed to be little stress
Unless I lost a sheep
Even that could be an adventure
Hunting and finding him
Maybe stuck in a sewer grate
The sheep and I both happy when I found him
I figured I could shepherd for my whole life
It didn't seem like real work
I didn't think I would ever have to say
"Miss Stevens, get me the Fluffy file please"

I would have a covenant like in the Bible
I wasn't sure exactly what a covenant was
But it sounded like something
God would have with Abraham
And surely that would be a good thing

Singing kettle
Pavarotti to my ears
Aria for tea with family

Every summer newly-born deer
Don't yet know I mean no harm -
Still, I like to see them jump the fence

Canadian Shield boulder
Deposited here by glaciers years ago
Canada: home to hearty immigrants

Country roads
Take me home every summer
To where I uncovered me

Ride the high horse
Over the coarse hills
Ever so lightly

Reality is an acquired taste
Seeing everything as just that
Takes time, depending on how long we overdosed
On fake news

Zen doesn't change you
It provides a route
To uncover your true Buddha-nature
In 1903 a young Albert Einstein
Took a job in the Swiss patent office
He worked in the evenings and on the weekend
Publishing four ground-breaking Physics papers in 1905
His fellow workers paid little attention to him
They saw in him what they expected to see
A rather dweebish government employee
Not unlike themselves
A variety of educational facilities
Provided him with a route
To uncover the remarkable mind
Of the greatest theoretical physicist
Since Isaac Newton
Should his fellow workers meet him on the street
Years later
They would be surprised not by his fame and fortune
But that despite this, he remained a rather dweebish government employee
His genius, his accomplishments, his Nobel Prize, his status
Didn't change Albert the man
Nor does Zen
Before *satori* mountains are mountains
And rivers are rivers
As one's practise deepens
The graphic insight that mountains and rivers
Are in a state of flux
An expression of their Buddha-nature
Consequently, mountains are not mountains
And river are not rivers
This discovery is illuminating and sometimes enlightening
After enlightenment
Mountains return to simply being mountains
And rivers, to being rivers
This is the contradiction of enlightened reality
Everything changes - Nothing changes

The Path circles back to where it started
But now you see that again, for the first time
In truth, Nothing happened

You will see
What you expect to see
Through glasses
Colored by your own experience

It is the root that nurtures the tree
Forget the branches
Get to the root

A monk went to see a Zen master
The master struck him
"Ow," cried the monk. "Why did you hit me?
I haven't opened my mouth yet!"
The master replied, "I don't have the time to wait"

A true poem
Is one that appears on the page
While you were sharpening your pencil

Sit comfortably with
The don't-know-mind
This is the fire that forges the finest steel

True happiness
Is impossible -
If you think about it

As I walk around my neighborhood
I say hello to almost everyone I encounter
Many I know - We have lived here
For more than twenty years
Even if I don't know them
They may still be neighbors
And if they are not even neighbors
So what? They are human beings
Fellow social animals
As such they warrant at least a smile
Which they may pass on
Sometimes when I meet a stranger
And he moves to his left to let me pass
As I move to my right to let him pass
And then we both reverse the move
We laugh
I may say, "Sorry I don't have time to dance"
I know, I know it's not exactly Seinfeld
But often his reply is spot on
And we both laugh
This is an example of humans being human
It reaffirms our connectedness
Our mutual humanity
Our shared Buddha-natures
Strangers are truly just friends
We haven't met yet
We don't know what issues they are dealing with
Perhaps a smile or a laugh
A human touch
May be just what they needed
To tip them out of some funk
In which they found themselves
I am Tipperman

What is the difference
Between a monk and a lay person?
Only laity ask that question

When you sit on your cushion
Shikantaza - just sit
Don't wander all over the place

For forty years
I have been selling water
On the bank of a river
Stupid me! Ha-ha

Live with a quiet zest
For the miracle of small things
Windy winter day - snow falling down
And going back up

Zen allows me
To lose my head
While everyone else
Is keeping theirs

Question only your questions
They lead to more questions -
Drinking salty water dehydrates

Ego sum pauper homo
Habeo nihil
Nihil opus est
I am a poor man
I have nothing
I am a rich man
I need nothing

❧

I have a beautiful wife
And two sons
And dear friends
Around the world
And right next door
Yet I spend much of my days
Alone and in silence
I am grateful to all these people
Who understand
All my love
Comes from
These silent and slow times

❧

I once asked
A house painter
If he was still learning anything
About painting
"After twenty years on the job
I am beginning to understand
How to do it."
A true craftsman
A second Michelangelo

The greatest truth
Is pain
Your attention seldom flags
When tears abound

With Zen
Even if you are not sure
Where you are going
It doesn't mean
You are not getting there

Zen is the ultimate example
Of Occam's razor -
The simplest answer is best

The Buddha never spoke first
He waited for a query
He was a first responder

If your ego
Always get what it wants
You have learned nothing

The angels come and go
Playing harps
With no strings attached

One man said
"I sweat all day long
For little pay"
His friend added
"I move large boulders
For even less pay"
A third man declared
"...And I am building
A cathedral!"

❧

The Buddha said the truth is
Sanditthiko
Akaliko
Ehipassiko
Opanayiko
Paccatam veritabbo vinnuhi
Here and now
Timeless
Come and see
Leaning inwards
Only known through direct experience

❧

Shoot an arrow
Into the sky
At each precise
Micro moment
The arrow is not moving
As if captured
By a Nikon
In the next
Micro moment
It is again
Motionless

But clearly it has moved
The arrow moves
The arrow is motionless
Both are right
Both are wrong

Even Buddhists
Can converse
With angels
Who studied with Duolingo

It is the dawning
Of the age of miracles
And wonders -
The falling of snow on a moonlit night

Poetry can only point
To the moon
It cannot be the moon
Even if the poet
Has been to the moon

"It's complicated"
May be the only cliche
True on every occasion

I am an ecstatic pessimist
I extract joy
From the cesspool of life

I am too old now
To be other than I am
I am past my best before date
Too late to pretend to be someone else...
Finally

I bonded with my father on the water
He liked to fish
I liked to be with him
I like to sit in the boat
And listen to the lapping
Of the water on the hull.
I would drop my line overboard
Even though it had no bait
I liked to fish
Except for the baiting of the hook
With a live worm
And extricating said hook
From the fish's mouth
If by chance I was unlucky enough
To actually entice a fish to bite
We both liked the early morning
Peace and quiet
We both liked the hunt
Every now and then
Dad would suggest
We try a different spot
Closer to shore
In a cove
As if he was a fish-whisperer
Who picked up messages
From the navigator of the school
We were tracking
We never caught a fish
But we went out every morning
I loved that my dad never called me out
For not baiting my line
But the question remained
Why did he continue when it was obvious
He was never going to bring home breakfast
It took me many years but now I think I know the answer
My dad didn't want to catch a fish
He wanted to fish

He couldn't go out in the boat and just sit
So, he went through the motions
He didn't call me on my hook-less line
Because he was doing the same thing I was doing
Bonding, and for that I loved him even more

Getting rid of the excess baggage
Of the ego -
Do not replace it with a Zen carry-on

                                                Only still water
                                                 Can reflect
                                                  The stars

With Zen you begin to recognize
The joy of the mundane familiar
You know your life is not real
But yet, you live it as if it is

                              Zen can make you so exasperated
        (Who cares what the sound of one hand clapping is anyway?)
                          That you stop pretending to be you

There are no secret teachings
You know all the answers
Just refrain from asking the wrong question -
Especially if you know every question is the wrong one

                                      Mentor or tormentor?
                               It doesn't make any difference
                        Whatever it takes to facilitate awakening

As the defilements calm
As the Buddha-nature reveals itself
The mind opens to the Dharmadhatu
The energy of the body of Dharma truth
Which melds with the receptivity
In the individual mind
This tying together of the individual mind
With the universal consciousness
Is the very definition of *yoga*
Which is a Sanskrit word meaning yoke
You are not alone in your quest
The Dharmadhatu is a force for good
It brought St. Paul to his knees
On the road to Damascus
It allowed Jesus to walk on water
And feed the multitudes
It helped Moses part the Red Sea
It inspired Socrates to teach
And stay strong to his convictions
It aids and abets various seekers

Different cultures, religions, and spiritual beliefs
Express it in their own way
In the end all agree
It is a universal vibration of truthful awareness
Protecting genuine seekers
From doubt and fear
Helping your innate Buddha-nature
To be fully realized
Traveling beyond life and death,
Stepping off the wheel of Samsara.
Protecting you from the pernicious forces of Mara
As long as your intentions are pure
You can rest assured
That no harm will come to you

My children used to be
Afraid of the dark
Now I am concerned
They may be
 Afraid of the light

                                        The poor don't have much
                                           But the greedy
                                         Don't have anything

The rats
Chewed a hole in my woven shawl -
Now I feel the warm breeze

                                              Your duty -
                                    Ease the load of others
                                   With kindness and grace
                                      Listen to their story
                                     For it is your story too

Leonard Cohen apparently never said the "F" word
Finally, one thing we have in common
He with wealth, fame, adoring fans,
Charisma, and a multitude of awards
Leaving nothing for me
Bless him for taking that load on himself

                               My sister is a born-again Christian
                               She is still waiting for her miracle
                                   She has never lost her faith
                                Perhaps that is her miracle

Zen allows you to get sidetracked
Blocked and at times frustrated
Until after years
You're still wailing against the darkness
Not going gentle into anything
You're tired and fed up
Because there is no other path
So, you buckle down and just sit
As long as it takes
But still without knowing why
Without any hope for success
Call it blind faith
Call it faint hope
Call it a hail Mary
In the fading moments of the game
Good, finally you got the point
Now you're ready to start

In the Himalaya of northern India
Lies the Tibetan village
Of Dharamshala
One evening
I attended a small concert
Mostly for the expat community
From the four corners of the world
Brought there to breathe in the same air
As the 14th Dalai Lama
Who lives nearby
We were a small crowd
Mostly providing technical assistance
To the Tibetan band that was to perform
Their first song was Neil Young's "Helpless"
They sang
"There is a town in north Ontario
All my changes were there"

Everyone started to sing along
Everyone knew the words
We all sang in unison
I gazed out the window at the mountains
And at the maroon-robed monks walking by
The whole world united in that moment by a song
Maybe it was the dawning of the Age of Aquarius after all

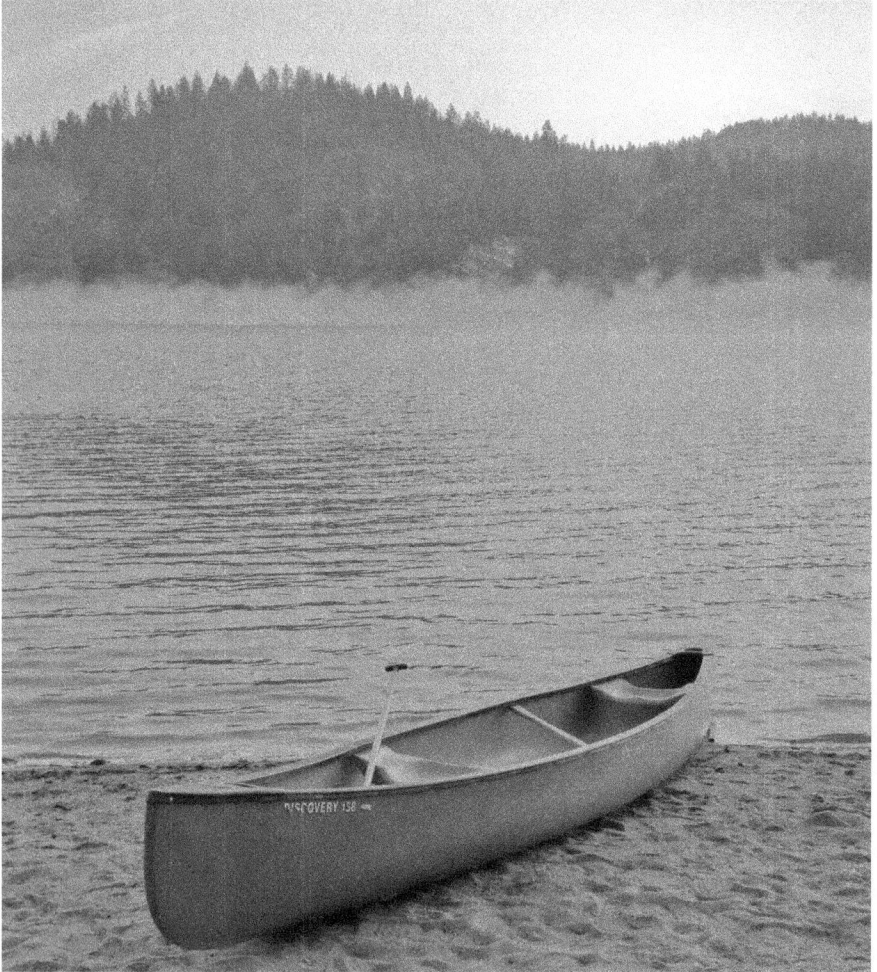

With Zen
You know more
Than you can enunciate

We don't practise Zen
We set aside some quiet time
To hone focus and patience

Midnight on the lake
My empty canoe
Filled with moonlight

Move past the past
Face the future when it is now
Stand here, alive and ready

Maezumi's three admonitions
Don't deceive yourself
Don't make excuses for yourself
Take responsibility for yourself

The Dhamma abides
In the rainbow
And in the thunderstorm

Most people inhabit space
Two weeks removed from today
Either in the past or in the future
Today does not exist except to
Bemoan past turmoil and shortcomings
Or to hope that tomorrow if not evermore
Will be better
As my mother used to say,
"Happy holidays...now
If we can just get through Christmas."

Eternal salvation?
This is not the path for you
The Buddha can't save you
He points the way
Outlines the steps needed
And personifies the outcomes
You and you alone are responsible
For your own salvation
You got yourself into this mess
Only you can free yourself.
As my mother used to say
"It serves you right"

It is an honor
To practise Zen
In the manner of the Buddha
To sit with elegance
To sit with grace
To sit with patience
Respecting the teachings
Preserved and clarified
By the disciples and teachers

To whom we pay our respects
By seeking refuge
In the Buddha
In the Dhamma
In the Sangha
I honor the Triple Gem

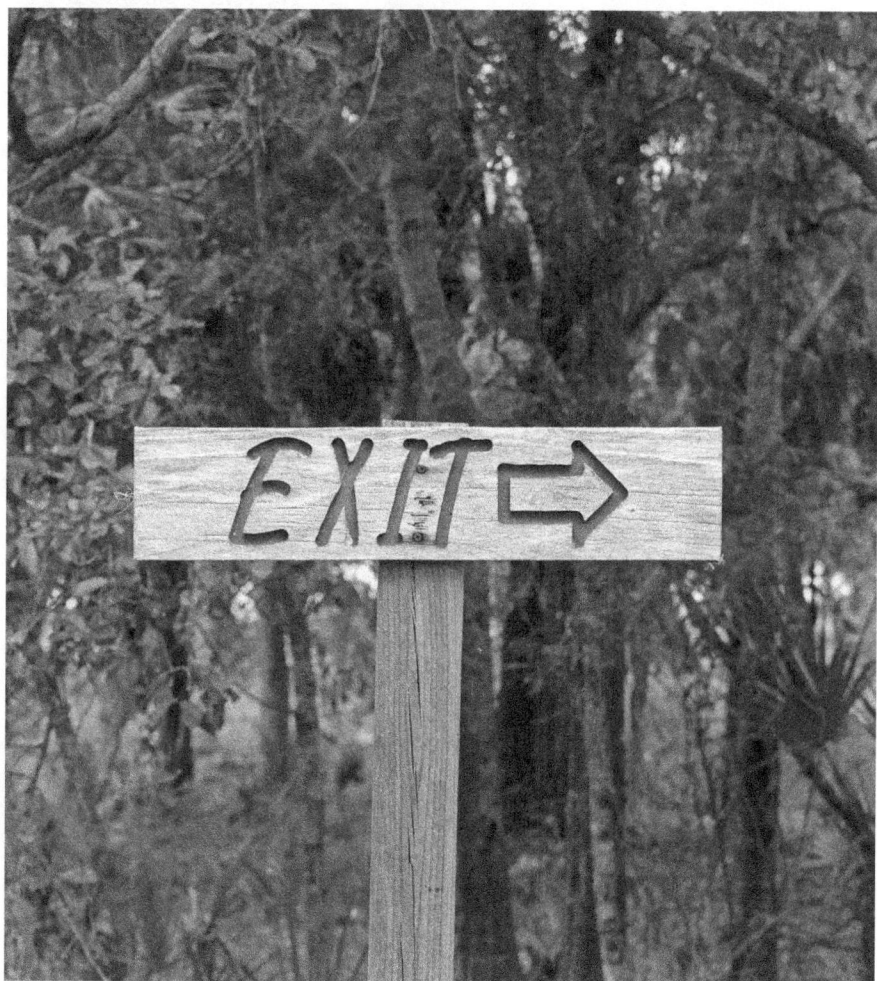

Zen, if nothing else
Is a relief
Maintaining a persona
With its supporting lifestyle
Demands arduous buffing and tweaking
Zen welcomes the person you always were
Before you were born

Freedom is paramount
What good is constitutionally-guaranteed liberty
If we are forever enslaved by our conditioning

Living in the present
Is to be fully aware
Of the heartbeat of the universe

Everything from pain to elation
Is just that
Over spicing whatever has arisen
All we taste is the oregano

At the lake you never know
What you might find floating
In your morning coffee
And yet, still you drink it

Even not to choose
Is to choose
The road forks, as it does eternally
Now what?

The propellant of a thought
Is feeling
Accelerating this strengthened thought
To leapfrog into our consciousness
Ahead of so many other thoughts

❦

I visited Versailles years ago
I remember nothing about it
Not even the smell of the crowds
All I can say today is
"I think I visited Versailles"
Much of my travels is the same
"I think I've been to Chiang Mai
Or was it Chiang Rai or Miami"
Makes me wonder what all the fuss was
We have to go there
See this, eat here, climb this, swim that,
Travels on camels, trains, rickshaws and tuk-tuks
Take pictures now stored in boxes
Endless smiling faces standing in front of...
Wait, who is that anyway?
We'll have the memories
We've been told
Now I can't remember my memories
I might as well have stayed home
And had a nice cup of tea in the garden

❦

"Diversions" a Saturday-only
Section of my newspaper
Speaks volumes about modern life
Diversions from what exactly?
Boredom? Fear? Loneliness?
Remorse? Envy? Doubt?

These are the very marrow of human existence
They could be the stimulant
Not for escape into or surrender to
The darkening morass but for
Introspection, investigation, insights
And basic questioning about
What precisely is it all about

To endeavor to speak the truth
Is to inadvertently tell a lot of lies

                                        Zen and quantum physics
                                        Both declare that any thing is
                                    Not the same but not different either

Split rail fence built long ago
Dividing the earth in two
Lies rotting today under weathered leaves
And storm-broken branches
Setting the earth aright -
Not two, not one

                                        The right view about Zen
                                        Is to acquaint the mind
                                        Moment after moment
                                        With *anicca* impermanence

It takes years of practise
To discover
There is no need to practise

                                        You have been shackled
                                        Only by your belief
                                        That you can't be free

Munindra-ji was very clear
"The dharma means living the life fully"
Ask yourself what is stopping me
From living my life fully
Trying to do this by sitting
On a cushion all day long
Is like trying to master Liszt
Only by playing scales
From dawn to dusk
To live a full life, you need not change it
You need not wear different clothes
You need not display your mala beads
You need not change your job
You need not take a vow of poverty
Simply live the life
With all its pain, joy, fear, craving and confusion
Hold it all before the mind's eye
And smile

꽃

Compassion without wisdom
Is called idiot compassion
It is easy to practise
You can never be wrong
Your beatific smile
Your correctly colored T-shirt
With matching ribbon
Perhaps indicating
You are more concerned
With how others perceive you
Than any oppressed people
Whom you seek to support

꽃

We like and want
What we like and want
What we like and want
Doesn't like and want us in return
It is destined to be a one-sided love affair
The teaching of the Buddha helps us
Not to fall for the actress on the screen
This is a vicious circle
It is *vatta*. It is empty.

Where does your grief go
When you aren't obsessing about it?

In Mumbai, lying ill
My bed, my entire world -
Sustained by friends and greasy pakoras

Shunryu Suzuki said,
"Everything is perfect and
We can all use a little improvement"

There is only great emptiness
Nothing holy

When you let go
It is not the impediment
That is forever gone
But your attachment
To that impediment

Sometimes just bearing witness is enough
Until from the calm abiding
Comes a response, honest and true

The teachings of the Buddha
Do not need to be engaged
There is no need to display
The depth of your conviction
Open a bakery, a hospice, a homeless shelter
If you are moved to do so
If you do it for self-aggrandizement
To set a standard of involvement for others to follow
If you solicit donations
You have lost your way
Zen is unengaged with worldly Dhammas like
Success and failure
Happiness and failure
Praise and blame
Honor and shame

Zen is not a spiritual practise
It is not ethereal, esoteric, other-worldly
It is not an escape
Nor an end run around problems
It is grounded in the here and now
Of the real world
As this being is experiencing it
Right now, my bottom hurts when I sit
My head hurts when I stand up
My knee hurts when I walk
I have a toothache and tinnitus in one ear
I don't feel very holy
But I sure feel

To really be at peace
You don't need to win the battle
You need to disengage

A true artist
Doesn't talk of his art
He talks of his craft

After decades of Zen
I am certain of only one thing
Everything is uncertain

Freedom is not an easy choice
Many prefer the safety and comfort
Of a repetitive work environment
Fearful of casting off without a map or a paddle

I was born a Christian
But only on my parents' side

Every moment you are born again
The old you sheds its skin
With your next breath
Prepare yourself to be filled with infinite grace

The key is sustained awareness
Of the commuter train of conditioned thoughts
And their subsequent emotional reaction
The silence of awareness leaves
The conditioned thought-feeling
As just that. Nothing more
This silence of awareness,
The ability of the mind
To observe itself.
Is always there
Like the sun on a cloudy day

❦

Everyone wants to be happy
Because there is suffering
There is pain
With birth there is tears
Continuing through aging,
Illness and finally death
It is no wonder
Everyone wants to be happy.
Happiness seems to be cool lemonade
On a hot day.
But if it weren't so hot
We wouldn't need that lemonade
Likewise, if we didn't suffer
If we deeply understood it
We wouldn't need to be happy
We'd be content
We'd be tranquil
We'd see everything as just that
No need to crave or fear or hate anything
The Buddha outlined the path
To get rid of suffering
To resolve the pain of birth, old age, illness and death.

Some things are true but not right
Others are right but not true
Act and speak with this in mind

This from the Boss
"We take from our parents
And leave the rest"
A Buddha's insight
From the streets of New Jersey

At this moment
Every living person
Is immortal

Don't believe in miracles?
Ask a blind person
He will tell you, your sight is a miracle

Risk and failure still trumps
Inertia from fear of failing

Heavy monsoon rains
Village streets flooded -
Water buffaloes still standing still

There is no practise
And no secret teachings
Any special technique is an illusion
There is no good or bad, no heaven or earth
Just rain falling
On our parade
Constantly
There is no way around the storm
The route goes through the eye of the hurricane
What keeps us in equilibrium from all the buffeting
Is staying present to the conditioning
Calmly abiding
The slings and arrows of outrageous fortune
Knowing fully well everything is just that
And all the embellishments, commentaries,
Judging, hating and liking
Are conditioned reactions
To be feared perhaps, but inevitably transitory in nature
Makes life in its myriads of incarnations
Perfect

To get a lot of things done
Leads to a feeling of accomplishment
To leave some things undone
Leads to peace

It is a fallacy
To remain true to a self
That changes every moment
Any tragedy is less important
Than how you deal with it

If you don't believe in anything
Try at least to conjure up some suspicions

Calcutta Mail to Bodh Gaya
Sleeping two to a bunk
Chai wallas arrive five a.m.
A warm glass of sunrise.

What is the meaning of life?
On the summer deck
Early morning oriole trillings
Bird droppings in your coffee

What is the most important part of Zen?
Getting out of bed

Eighty-year-old Hey Sol
Arrived in the rehab unit
Due to a concussion from a fall.
She was unsteady on her feet
And her speech was slurred
The nurses administered appropriate medications
At the appropriate times
In the appropriate manner
They helped her to take a shower every day
And every day she put on the same frayed burgundy T-shirt
She had been wearing since her arrival
She refused, politely, to change it.
By the fifth day the nurses
Asked this otherwise mild-mannered patient, why?
Why every day?
She explained "My husband
Is ninety-nine years old
He can't leave our home
We have been married for sixty years
I miss him so much
It is his favorite T-shirt"
The nurses nodded and then smiled
And asked her if she wanted
Coffee with her dinner

Zen is like standing on your head
Easy to conceptualize
Challenging to do
Impossible to sustain

Do not be a seriously devoted student
Do the work.
No need to show off

Age quod agis -
Concentrate on the task at hand -
When eating, just eat
When reading, just read
When reading while eating
Just reading while eating

I cannot crave
For the gold watch
On my wrist

See the significant
As trivial
And the insignificant
As formidable

No end to practise
No beginning to enlightenment
Zen is all path

The Buddha gave 84,000 discourses
Outlining the human condition
The following comes close
In just twenty lines...
A Jewish mother brought her son
To the sea side to play on the beach
The sea was quite rough that day
And a large wave
Carried the boy far out to sea
The mother was distraught
She fell to her knees and prayed
"Dear Lord I beg you
Return my son to me
He is all I have
I will return to the Synagogue
Make penance and live a holy life
Devoted to good deeds
I will praise your beneficence to all!"
With that another large wave
Arrived on the shore
Depositing the boy in its wake on the beach
The mother gathered her drenched son in her arms
With tears of joy she looked to heaven
And said, "He had a hat."

Using your intellect to reach the truth
Is like scratching an itch
With your boot on

                                        No thinker, no thinking
                                    Just thoughts passing through
                                     On the way to the trash can

Reality is just that
We impose our ego into it
Judging it as thus and so
And we suffer accordingly

                                        Find some small solace
                                        Just bearing witness
                                          Casting a lifeline
                                          To a sunken hull

Awareness is simply knowing
That something happened
Tulku Urgyen Rinpoche
Calls it "empty cognizance"

                                        The present is always
                                        Right here, right now
                                        Except when the mind
                                        Is otherwise disposed

There
That is enough
There have been too many words already
I have said what I wanted to say
So many times over
I am losing my voice
The time has come to be quiet
And so, I lay down my pen
Look. Over there
A red rose of a cardinal
On the snow-filled window sill

On second thought, one last story....

(1)
We were living in Toronto
One summer
In my grandma's one bedroom apartment
On Avenue Road below St. Claire
We were my mother, my sister and I
For a total of four
It was crowded and hot
The traffic outside was incessant
I was ten years old
I slept in the living room by myself
The single small bedroom was shared
By the female contingent
I didn't know their sleeping arrangement
But I did know there was no second bed.
At bedtime my mother covered
The blue corduroy couch in the living room
With a pink bed sheet
And put a matching pillow case
On the cushion.
I felt very bohemian

Very urban and urbane
We left the balcony door open
To the sounds of the big city
I loved it
But I also loved staying
At Wyldwood
My Mother's sister's forty-acre estate
Outside Toronto
We each would get our own bedroom
With attached bath
We ate breakfast in the breakfast room
Imagine, a separate room just for toast!
We dressed for dinner
And ate in the formal dining room
My Uncle Jack sat at the head of the table
He did the carving, the table so long
We had to pass the filled plates to each other
It was there that I learned not to reach
We said grace
Uncle Jack always ending with
"Go easy on the butter, boys,
It's twenty cents a pound."

(2)
One day that summer
I arranged to go to the movies with a friend
After which Aunt Dorothy would pick us up
And we would all go to Wyldwood
For a few days
Grandma would remain at the apartment
Perfect
The mesmerizing movie
Pushed the upcoming trip to my Aunt's
Into the dark recessed netherworld
Of my childhood brain
My friend and I were so engrossed

In our discussion of the finer nuances
Of the destruction and mayhem of the movie
That we decided to walk home
A much longer journey than by subway
By the time I arrived home
Full of anticipation
I walked in to a very quiet apartment
Grandma trundled out of the bedroom
To inform me mom had waited as long as she could
I would have to stay with grandma
I was catatonic. I felt abandoned.
Surely, they would realize their mistake
Any minute now the door would open
And there would stand my mother
Arms outstretched saying
"I'm so sorry. We made a terrible mistake
Grab your pajamas and let's go"
Grandma and I had a very quiet dinner.
I sulked, I pouted. I sniffled.
Then she suggested we play cards.
We played Euchre, a game from back in the pioneer times
Grandma kept winning, piling up the points
She was very good. She seemed to be enjoying herself
Slowly I caught on to the game
I won a trick. Then another
This was more like it. The game was kind of fun
Grandma kept score
Sometime later she informed that we were tied
So maybe I should go to bed
I begged her to keep playing
"Okay," she said. "Just don't tell your mother how late you stayed up."
We played and laughed and played some more and I got to stay up real late
and
We played some more and she made up my bed and kissed me good night
"Don't worry," she said. "Your mother will be home soon."
"Who?" I said, and we both laughed.

The end

ABOUT PARIYATTI

Pariyatti is dedicated to providing affordable access to authentic teachings of the Buddha about the Dhamma theory (*pariyatti*) and practice (*paṭipatti*) of Vipassana meditation. A 501(c)(3) nonprofit charitable organization since 2002, Pariyatti is sustained by contributions from individuals who appreciate and want to share the incalculable value of the Dhamma teachings. We invite you to visit www.pariyatti.org to learn about our programs, services, and ways to support publishing and other undertakings.

Pariyatti Publishing Imprints

Vipassana Research Publications (focus on Vipassana as taught by S.N. Goenka in the tradition of Sayagyi U Ba Khin)

BPS Pariyatti Editions (selected titles from the Buddhist Publication Society, copublished by Pariyatti)

MPA Pariyatti Editions (selected titles from the Myanmar Pitaka Association, copublished by Pariyatti)

Pariyatti Digital Editions (audio and video titles, including discourses)

Pariyatti Press (classic titles returned to print and inspirational writing by contemporary authors)

Pariyatti enriches the world by
- disseminating the words of the Buddha,
- providing sustenance for the seeker's journey,
- illuminating the meditator's path.

www.ingramcontent.com/pod-product-compliance
Lightning Source LLC
Chambersburg PA
CBHW031842090426
42741CB00005B/326